VOLU

OLD TES

THE NEW COLLEGEVILLE BIBLE COMMENTARY

WISDOM

Richard J. Clifford, S.J.

SERIES EDITOR

Daniel Durken, O.S.B.

LITURGICAL PRESS
Collegeville, Minnesota

www.litpress.org

Nihil Obstat: Reverend Robert Harren, Censor deputatus.
Imprimatur: ✠ Most Reverend John F. Kinney, J.C.D., D.D., Bishop of St. Cloud, Minnesota, October 12, 2012.

Design by Ann Blattner.

Cover illustration: Detail of Wisdom Woman by Donald Jackson. © 2007 The Saint John's Bible, Order of Saint Benedict, Collegeville, Minnesota. Used with permission. All rights reserved.

Photos: page 16, Wikimedia Commons; pages 28, 59, 69, and 80, Thinkstock Photos; page 48, Moses Strikes the Rock by James Jacques Tissot, at the Jewish Museum, New York, NY. Used with permission.

1   2   3   4   5   6   7   8   9

Library of Congress Cataloging-in-Publication Data

Clifford, Richard J.
    Wisdom / Richard J. Clifford, S.J. ; series editor, Daniel Durken, O.S.B.
      pages cm. — (New Collegeville Bible commentary. Old Testament ; volume 20)
    ISBN 978-0-8146-2854-6
      1. Bible. O.T. Apocrypha. Wisdom of Solomon--Commentaries.   I. Durken, Daniel.   II. Title.

BS1755.53.C59   2013
229'.3077—dc23

                                              2012035751

CONTENTS

ABBREVIATIONS

Books of the Bible

Acts—Acts of the Apostles
Amos—Amos
Bar—Baruch
1 Chr—1 Chronicles
2 Chr—2 Chronicles
Col—Colossians
1 Cor—1 Corinthians
2 Cor—2 Corinthians
Dan—Daniel
Deut—Deuteronomy
Eccl (or Qoh)—Ecclesiastes
Eph—Ephesians
Esth—Esther
Exod—Exodus
Ezek—Ezekiel
Ezra—Ezra
Gal—Galatians
Gen—Genesis
Hab—Habakkuk
Hag—Haggai
Heb—Hebrews
Hos—Hosea
Isa—Isaiah
Jas—James
Jdt—Judith
Jer—Jeremiah
Job—Job
Joel—Joel
John—John
1 John—1 John
2 John—2 John
3 John—3 John
Jonah—Jonah
Josh—Joshua
Jude—Jude
Judg—Judges
1 Kgs—1 Kings

2 Kgs—2 Kings
Lam—Lamentations
Lev—Leviticus
Luke—Luke
1 Macc—1 Maccabees
2 Macc—2 Maccabees
Mal—Malachi
Mark—Mark
Matt—Matthew
Mic—Micah
Nah—Nahum
Neh—Nehemiah
Num—Numbers
Obad—Obadiah
1 Pet—1 Peter
2 Pet—2 Peter
Phil—Philippians
Phlm—Philemon
Prov—Proverbs
Ps(s)—Psalms
Rev—Revelation
Rom—Romans
Ruth—Ruth
1 Sam—1 Samuel
2 Sam—2 Samuel
Sir—Sirach
Song—Song of Songs
1 Thess—1 Thessalonians
2 Thess—2 Thessalonians
1 Tim—1 Timothy
2 Tim—2 Timothy
Titus—Titus
Tob—Tobit
Wis—Wisdom
Zech—Zechariah
Zeph—Zephaniah

Wisdom

Name, author, and audience

The book is known in the Septuagint (the early Greek version of the Old Testament) as Wisdom of Solomon and in the Latin tradition as The Book of Wisdom. Though neither Solomon (nor any individual for that matter) is ever named in the book, the author assumes the persona of the tenth-century Israelite king renowned for his wisdom. The book presupposes that its readers are familiar with the biblical portrait of Solomon, the wise king in 1 Kings 2–11, especially chapters 3; 5:9-14; 10:1-10. The author of another book categorized as wisdom literature, Ecclesiastes (fourth century B.C.), also assumes the persona of Solomon in Ecclesiastes 1–2 without naming him.

The author is not named, as in many biblical and apocryphal books. The practice enhances a book's authority by linking it to a tradition; the author's task is making that tradition relevant to a contemporary audience. Solomon represented the wisdom tradition. Though the author is unknown, a few biographical details can nonetheless be inferred from the book. The author is obviously a Jew with a fierce pride in Judaism, in God's call of the Jews, and in the relevance of the biblical story. The place of composition is generally assumed to be Alexandria, the Egyptian seaport on the Mediterranean Sea, on the Western Delta at the mouth of a branch of the Nile River, about 130 miles north of Cairo. The city, planned by Alexander the Great (356–323 B.C.) and built a few years after his death, had a large Jewish community whose upper class would have nurtured and understood the complex ideas and language of the book. Though it seems that Jews of the time were not ordinarily admitted into the *gymnasium* to receive a Hellenistic education, the author must have been one of those allowed to study Greek literature, rhetoric, and philosophy. The author delights in virtuoso display, coining words, inventing arguments, and playing on biblical traditions. The author's project is similar to that of the prolific Jewish philosopher Philo of Alexandria (ca. 20 B.C.–A.D. 50). Philo likewise stood within the Jewish tradition of biblical study, was familiar with pagan learning, and interested in the spiritual dimension of individual life. Like Philo, the author of Wisdom of Solomon is confident in humans' capacity to know God and act virtuously, and confident too in the special vocation of Israel, whom God protects and endows with wisdom.

What audience does the author have in mind? Until recently, most scholars would have answered a Gentile audience, for they assumed that Judaism vigorously promoted itself in the Hellenistic world and that Jewish works written in Greek were part of that missionary effort. There are, to be sure, indications that many non-Jews found Judaism very attractive. Acts 13:16, for example, speaks of "those who fear God," "God-fearers" who were attracted to Judaism but stopped short of full conversion. And according to Wisdom 18:4, "the imperishable light of the law was to be given to the world." Recent scholarship, however, is divided on the issue, some feeling that the primary goal of Jewish literature written in Greek was to help Jews maintain and strengthen their identity and their faith in a pluralistic world, though they would not necessarily rule out apologetic and missionary goals as well.

It is likely that the primary audience envisioned by the book was Jewish, for only such an audience would have understood the esoteric commentary on the Bible and accepted the uncompromising monotheism and election of Israel as God's "son." The latter two teachings were contrary to the broad "philanthropic" outlook of educated pagans. Instruction of Jews was a necessity in the Hellenistic marketplace of ideas, for one could not assume young Jews would adopt the religion of their ancestors (see below). The biblical "base text" in Wisdom of Solomon is the wisdom books, especially the book of Proverbs. Like Ben Sira a century before within the Palestinian culture of Jerusalem, the author integrates those wisdom traditions with the historical books of the Bible, especially Exodus. The wisdom tradition, enriched with material from the historical books of the Bible, enabled both authors to deal with existential and national issues at one and the same time.

Date and place of composition

The book contains no specific historical references by which one can date it. The best evidence is literary; the affinities in phraseology and ideas with the writings of Philo of Alexandria suggest the authors were contemporaries in Alexandria (30 B.C.–A.D. 40). Specialized meanings of some words in Wisdom of Solomon match other writings of the period; tensions at the time between Jews and their urban neighbors would account for the book's concern with justice and its harsh criticism of Egyptian customs;

Wisdom of Solomon presupposes its readership is literate and thoroughly Hellenized, which would have been true of the large Jewish community at Alexandria. Alexandria was the capital of Egypt and a brilliant center of Hellenistic philosophy and art, which was symbolized by its famous museum and library. The Greek translation of the Hebrew Bible (the Septuagint) was, according to Jewish tradition, initiated by Ptolemy Philadelphus (285–246 B.C.) for the library. It is tempting to imagine that Wisdom of Solomon was written for such a vibrant community, where Jews would see the grandeur of their traditions depicted by an author skilled in Hellenistic rhetoric and philosophy as well as biblical lore.

Hellenistic Judaism

The Judaism reflected in Wisdom of Solomon is largely a product of Hellenistic culture rather than the Palestinian culture reflected in the Hebrew Bible. One should not, however, regard the two cultures as totally distinct, for each was multi-faceted and there was considerable overlap. "Hellenistic" is an adjective for Greek culture ("Hellenism") in its interaction with the native cultures of the East, an interaction initiated by Alexander the Great in the fourth century B.C. The age was the first great marketplace of ideas in the East. The old cultures and societies of the ancient East, ruled by tradition and custom, were confronted by new ideas, customs, and people. Two areas are especially relevant to this introduction—religion and philosophy. Enthusiastic advocates of the new religions traveled about expounding their views and looking for followers. The religions and philosophies were regarded as ways of life as well as doctrines; they were intellectual-ethical systems.

Of the many emphases of Hellenistic religion, three are especially important for Wisdom of Solomon. The first was miracles. Performing miracles was the mark of a god, and lists called aretalogies were kept of a god's miracles. The religions were also interested in immortality as a gift from god. Pre-Hellenistic Judaism did not use the concepts of immortality or eternal life to express the blessed future. Rather, it looked for divine restoration of the nation as a whole. But in the Hellenistic marketplace, a good religion had to promise immortality. Even in Egypt, where life after death had always been offered, it was now offered to more people than before. A third feature of Hellenistic religions was the claim of great antiquity. A religion had to be old to have credibility, for new ideas required validation by the tried and the true. Several ancient events were cited as standards of antiquity: the reign of Semiramis, the legendary founder of Assyria; the Trojan War, the oldest datable event in Greek history; and the Flood.

The above emphases appear in Wisdom of Solomon. Wisdom 11–19 portrays the central biblical event of the exodus as a series of miracles in which natural elements change their properties. Immortality is the dominant category of hope, which is a striking difference from earlier biblical books. As examples of antiquity, Wisdom of Solomon presents Adam as the first person guided by wisdom (10:1); among its heroes is Noah "when . . . the earth was flooded" (10:4-5). The author knows what attracts followers. What is most important, however, is that the author of Wisdom has entered the marketplace of ideas with the aim of persuading fellow Jews of the relevance of their Jewish faith.

Philosophical influences

Wisdom of Solomon engaged the same questions as the philosophies of the day, incorporating without apology whatever elements might make the biblical tradition more meaningful and credible to a Jewish audience. Ben Sira, the author of the book of Sirach, another piece of wisdom literature in the Old Testament, in an earlier century borrowed some concepts from Stoicism (e.g., Sir 41:14–42:8; 43:27; 36:1-4), but to a much lesser degree than this author. The principal Hellenistic philosophical movements were Stoicism, Epicureanism, and Skepticism. All were rooted in the great philosophical schools of the fourth century B.C., Plato's Academy and Aristotle's Lyceum. A widely-used division of the period shows that philosophy was conceived more broadly and integrally than in the modern West: logic (the study of reasoning and discourse), physics (the study of external nature), and ethics (the study of human nature and how life ought to be lived). All the schools agreed that philosophy was a serious affair and had the purpose of gaining life-enhancing wisdom.

Of these three schools, Stoicism was influential on Wisdom of Solomon. In physics, it was materialist, rejecting external entities such as Plato's forms and Aristotle's unmoved mover (God) as explanations of sensible reality and of motion. In ethics, it was strongly rationalist; happiness is attained by the right use of reason, and moral failures are failures in the functioning of reason. The most important philosophical influence on Wisdom of Solomon, however, was Middle Platonism (ca. 80 B.C.–A.D. 250), which is the scholarly designation of the Platonic tradition from the first century to the third century A.D. Shapers of the tradition included several Alexandrians—Philo and the church fathers Clement (ca. A.D. 150–215) and Origen (A.D. 185–254). Elements of Stoicism and Aristotelianism had by this time become part of the Platonic tradition. Middle Platonism became increasingly a metaphysical or theological system, characterized, among other things, by ideas as thoughts in the mind of God, assimilation to God as an ideal of human life, and the hierarchy of being.

Aspects of Stoicism and Middle Platonism are found in popularized form in Wisdom of Solomon, especially in Wisdom 13–15. Examples of general Greek influence are the four virtues in Wisdom 8:7 (the Christian "cardinal" virtues), temperance, prudence, justice, and fortitude, and the viewing of fire, wind, stars, or water as animating forces in the world (13:2). Stoic influence is seen in the use of the concept of a world soul (7:24), materialist physics (8:1; 19:18), the proof from design (13:1), and the mode of argument called the *sorites* (chain argument) in 8:17-21. Borrowings from Middle Platonism include the pre-existence of souls (8:19), the sharp distinction between body and soul (8:20; 9:15), and the diminished reality of the material world compared to the spiritual world of heaven (9:15-16).

The author draws on one or another philosophical tenet without necessarily fully subscribing to the system of which they are a part. An example is the immortality of the soul (Wis 3:1-4), which in the book is a prelude to the establishment of the kingdom of God (see below).

The genre and the structure of the book

The genre of the book has been much debated. Indeed some scholars have even denied the book is a unity. In recent decades, a number of scholars have proposed that the book belongs to a type of literature mentioned in classical rhetorical treatises though no complete example has survived—the elaborate commendation of a way of life (which is sometimes called a protreptic). The author faced a situation unparalleled in Judaism—an educated community that required persuasion to *choose* afresh their ancestral traditions amid the clamor of competing and prestigious opportunities.

In recent decades, a consensus has formed about the broad structure of the book. The book has three parts: Part 1: 1:1–6:21, the depiction by means of typical figures and events of the authentic (though hidden) world and the justice that characterizes its governance; Part 2: 6:22–10:21, the gift of wisdom that enables one to understand this world and live happily in it; and Part 3: 11:1–19:22, the exodus as the great illustration of how the world operates. Ancient manuscripts were not provided with the visual guides of modern printed books. It was the responsibility of the author rather than copyists to indicate the structure. Authors used repetitions of key words to frame sections by using them at the beginning and end of a passage. This is called *inclusio*. The outline below, reflecting the consensus of biblical scholars, is a convenient guide to a complex and dense book. Some of the units below are marked by *inclusio* and the structure is chiastic. In a chiasm the elements are repeated in reverse, resulting in the pattern ABBA. It is common in ancient literature.

Part 1 (1:1–6:21) The Two Worlds

A. Exhortation to pagan kings: Rule according to divine justice and seek wisdom! (1:1-11)

   B. A drama in which the true nature of the world is revealed (1:12–2:24)

      C. Contrasting portraits: death of the just and impious (3–4)

   B'. Divine judgment against the wicked and for the righteous person (5:1-23)

A'. Repetition of the exhortation to pagan kings: Rule according to divine justice and seek wisdom! (6:1-21).

Part 2 (6:22–10:21) Wisdom and the Way to It

Wisdom 6:22-25 introduces the themes. Wisdom 6:22–8:21 is composed of seven passages.

A. The origin of the wise king is like any other human (7:1-6)

   B. I, Solomon, prayed for wisdom (7:7-12)

      C. Giving of wisdom of God to Solomon (7:13-22a; vv. 13b and 21a have an *inclusio* around "hide" and "hidden")

         D. Praise of wisdom—its nature, origin, and attributes (7:22b–8:1)

      C'. Solomon will marry wisdom who lives with God (8:2-9)

   B'. Thoughts of the young king (8:10-16)

A'. Young Solomon will ask for wisdom (8:17-21; vv. 17b and 21d, *inclusio*: "heart")

Chapters 7 and 8 prepare for the prayer at their beginning (7:7) and end (8:21). The Prayer of Solomon in chapter 9 has three parts: vv. 1-6 about human beings, vv. 7-12 about Solomon, and vv. 13-18 about human beings. The prayer is the center of book because the beginning of the prayer is concerned with creation (theme of Part I) and the end is concerned with salvation (theme of Part II).

Chapter 10 presents the eight "wisdom heroes" of Genesis, each of whom is involved in a contrast. Abel is opposed to his brother Cain. All except Cain were helped by wisdom who came to their rescue. The reference to prayer in 10:20 is an *inclusio* of 19:9, the final verse of the book.

Part 3 (11:1–19:22) The Exodus: God Provides for His Child Israel

The exodus is viewed as seven "comparisons" (Greek: *synkrisis*, 11:1-14 and 16:1–19:22). The plagues against the Egyptians (given in italics below) are contrasted with the blessings given to the Israelites during the exodus (given in roman type below). The comparisons are interrupted by two digressions in verses 11:15–15:19.

Comparison 1. 11:6-14 *flowing water*—water from the rock

    Digression 1: the moderation of God in punishing the wicked, Egypt, and Canaan (11:15–12:27)

    Digression 2: a critique of idol worshipers (13:1–15:19)

Comparison 2. 16:1-4 *frogs*—quails

Comparison 3. 16:5-14 *flies and locusts*—bronze serpent

Comparison 4. 16:15-29 *storm and hail*—manna

Comparison 5. 17:1–18:4 *darkness*—light

Comparison 6. 18:5-25 *death of first-born*—Israel spared

Comparison 7. 19:1-9 *drowning in the Red Sea*—passage through the Red Sea

Final statement and broadening of the perspective (19:10-22).

The meaning of the book of Wisdom

By making Solomon the speaker and by building on the wisdom tradition, the author is employing the most universal and least nationalist part of the Bible. The appeal is to the nations (in the person of their kings), especially in 1:1-15 and 6:1-21. Though the envisioned audience is primarily Jewish, the book addresses Gentile rulers in these passages; the same dynamic is found in Psalm 2 and Isaiah 40–55. They are called to recognize the just God's governance of the world and the coming judgment that was part of that governance. In part 2 (6:22–10:21) Solomon appears as the model king and seeker after wisdom. Thereafter Israel is the protected and wise "son/child" of God (part 3, 10:22–19:22). The universalist outreach of the wisdom literature has been enriched and qualified by the special role of Israel. Israel is a witness to the world of God's justice and protection.

Wisdom of Solomon seeks to demonstrate the reality of the "kingdom of God," or, in other terms, the sovereignty of Israel's Lord. To many Jews, that sovereignty was hidden in the sense that it was not yet fully realized and visible. Non-Jews denied the rule of Israel's God, like the gang in Wisdom 2 who say " by mere chance were we born" (2:2). They kill the righteous person, God's child (2:20); only at the judgment do they see the resurrection of the child and the reality of the "kingdom" or sovereignty of God (Wis 5). In Wisdom of Solomon, knowledge of "the kingdom" does not consist merely in an intellectual appreciation of the Lord's universal dominion. Rather, the book expresses the concrete hopes of Jews in the period at the turn of the era. Like many in Judaism, the author seems to regard Israel to be still in exile, awaiting the fullness of redemption. Jewish literature both in the Diaspora and Palestine attests to the deep and widespread conviction that the national story has not yet come to its proper conclusion. Psalm 106:47 expresses a widespread feeling: "Save us, LORD, our God; / gather us from among the nations." Another biblical book awaiting the restoration of Israel is Daniel, written during the Maccabean crisis in the mid-second century B.C. Daniel 12:2-3 also viewed restoration as resurrection: "Many of those who sleep / in the dust of the earth shall awake; / Some to everlasting life, / others to reproach and everlasting disgrace. / But those with insight shall shine brightly / like the splendor of the firmament, / and those who lead the many to justice / shall be like the stars forever." Wisdom of Solomon has the same spirit (e.g., Wis 3:6-8; 4:16–5:2). Wisdom 3:7-8 seems to allude to the Daniel text and says of the just who have been slain that "they shall judge nations and rule over peoples, / and the LORD shall be their king forever." The resurrection of the dead in Wisdom 5 seems to refer to the same intermediate state as Daniel, where the righteous who have died await the restoration of Israel and the full realization of the reign of God.

The teaching on immortality (Greek: *athanasia*, 3:4; 4:1; 8:13, 17; 15:3) and incorruptibility (6:18, 19) must be understood in the same context of the judgment preceding restoration. Though the book borrows the Platonic language of the immortality of the soul, the context is completely different. For one thing, the author is primarily concerned with the Lord's governing rather than with an individual soul's reward. For another, the governing has a historical context—the restoration of Israel who, the author believes, is still in exile.

Three affirmations of the book have a special resonance for modern Christians. The first is its distinctive understanding of the kingdom (sovereignty) of God, which is perhaps the most persistent theme of the Bible. God's justice actually rules the world even though human kings are under the impression they have the final say. Divine wisdom is required to see divine justice at work. Such wisdom is (paradoxically) granted only to those who earnestly seek it. Though operative now, divine justice is not yet visible to the world. It becomes visible when God's "son" (2:18; 12:21; 16:10, 26; 18:4; also rendered "child" in 2:13; 16:21; 19:6 and "servant" in 12:7) is faithful to his "father" (2:16; 11:10). Fidelity means allowing the justice of God to work. Israel is God's child and thus witnesses to the true King of the universe. From its very founding in the exodus, Israel was protected, its enemies punished, and God was revealed as Lord of the universe.

God's lordship is not timeless, however. Israel does not live outside of history. For the author, the Lord had not finished regathering Israel from its exile. The critical time of refounding the community is approaching. Divine rule has been hidden in that it has not yet appeared in its fullness. There are now, therefore, "two worlds," corresponding in a sense to the two ways in ancient wisdom literature. One world is all too familiar, for its law is that might makes right and that those faithful to God are at risk from violent and selfish people. It is ruled over by the kings of this world. Though the other world has not appeared fully, it is destined to last; it is eternal, for it is ruled by God. Each world has its adherents, its citizens. The citizens of this world are doomed, however, as their world is passing away. The citizens of the true world already possess eternal life, for their world will endure.

The real world is marked by life and the other is marked by death. Paradoxically, it is when the righteous are faithful and rescued that the real world appears. In part 1, the death of the (typical) righteous person who trusts in God shows forth the true world when God raises up that person in the sight of those who killed him. In part 3, the justice of God is shown forth in the rescue of the "child" of God, Israel. As they are rescued in the sight of the Egyptians, the latter come to acknowledge the true God. The true world is revealed in the trusting and obedient conduct of the chosen ones.

A second contemporary issue is that God is Lord of the universe, which consists of nature and history. Many believers instinctively make God the Lord of heaven but retreat from affirming the lordship of earth, nature, and history. They have difficulty seeing God at work in the world, in human history, and are disposed to think separately of God acting in history and in nature. Wisdom of Solomon affirms the central reality of God the creator and of God's choice of Israel. God acts in history (in the book's perspective) primarily by dealing with Israel, reshaping at will human activity and natural elements. "For the elements, in ever-changing harmony, / like strings of the harp, produce new melody, / while the flow of music steadily persists" (19:18). To recognize this rule takes divine wisdom. It must be sought earnestly in prayer, preferred to all else, and yet, paradoxically, is conferred as a gift. Its possession enables one to see the true nature of reality and to remain faithful to it.

A third point relevant to Christian readers is the outreach of God that is called wisdom. Despite the author's learning in Greek philosophy, God is not portrayed as "the prime mover" or transcendent ideal. God is engaged in human history and dwells with the human race. At times, divine wisdom is the energy that runs through the universe; at other times, it is the inspiration that enters into human beings, directing them to act justly and trust in God's fatherly protection. Christian readers will see in this wisdom aspects of their triune God, which will be made more explicit in the pages of the New Testament and in subsequent Christian reflection.

Wisdom

THE TWO WORLDS

1:1–6:21

Part 1 of the book of Wisdom develops and combines two biblical traditions. The first is the view of world history found, among other places, in Psalms 2, 48, 89, 96; Isaiah 10:5-19; 44:24–45:7; 55; and Jeremiah 27, 29: the Lord, Most High over heavenly beings and earthly kings, directs the course of history, and the Lord's servant Israel is, in principle at least, similarly "most high" over the nations. Rulers of the earth are thus agents of the Lord and will be judged according to whether they ruled justly and wisely (Wis 1:1-15 and 6:1-21). Israel is privileged and protected, though explicitly identified as "your [the LORD's] children" only in part 3 (19:6). In part 1, the "child of the LORD" (2:13) is left unspecified. The second biblical tradition used in part 1 is the doctrine of "the two ways" (found especially in Proverbs and Psalms), which portrays the moral life in dramatic terms as walking on either of two opposed paths—the way of the righteous and the way of the wicked, each path having its proper destiny. Wisdom 1–6 shows the wicked (usually referring to a group) plotting against the righteous individual (Wis 2) and the respective destinies of each way (Wis 5). One of the "Two Worlds" in part 1 is the world of everyday experience. Ruled over by earthly kings, it is characterized by rampant wickedness and is short-lived. The other "world" is not always visible. Ruled over by the Lord, it is inhabited by the righteous who trust in God their Father (2:16). The true world becomes visible when the righteous act faithfully in the face of opposition, for God intervenes to rescue them. Divine intervention functions as a judgment that the righteous will live forever and the wicked will perish (Wis 5).

Part 1 is framed by exhortations to the rulers of the world in Wisdom 1:1-15 and 6:1-21. Couched in the language of personal relationship, the first exhortation warns the rulers (and their subjects) against inviting death through wickedness; the second exhortation urges them to court wisdom.

15

I. The Reward of Righteousness

**Exhortation to Righteousness,
the Key to Life**

1 ¹Love righteousness, you who judge
 the earth;
 think of the LORD in goodness,
 and seek him in integrity of heart;
²Because he is found by those who
 do not test him,
 and manifests himself to those
 who do not disbelieve
 him.
³For perverse counsels separate
 people from God,
 and his power, put to the proof,
 rebukes the foolhardy;

⁴Because into a soul that plots evil
 wisdom does not enter,
 nor does she dwell in a body
 under debt of sin.
⁵For the holy spirit of discipline flees
 deceit
 and withdraws from senseless
 counsels
 and is rebuked when unrighteous-
 ness occurs.

⁶For wisdom is a kindly spirit,
 yet she does not acquit blasphe-
 mous lips;
Because God is the witness of the
 inmost self
 and the sure observer of the heart
 and the listener to the tongue.

At chapter 6, the second exhortation is used to close this section and transition to the next.

1:1-15 Seek righteousness and wisdom to avoid death!

The instructions of Proverbs 1–9 urge the son or disciple to seek wisdom
above all. Though wisdom must be earnestly sought, it is ultimately a pure
gift of God. Wisdom brings life, which is defined as health, reputation,
wealth, a suitable spouse, and children. Its opposite, death arrives prematurely as punishment. Wisdom 1 develops these ideas from wisdom literature, especially Proverbs 8:15, "By me kings reign," and Proverbs 8:35-36,
"[Whoever] finds me finds life / . . . all who hate me love death." Wisdom
retains Proverbs' language of love and courtship as a metaphor of the search
for wisdom (see Wis 1:1, 12, 16).

The warning to "you who judge the earth" (Wis 1:1), as in Pss 2:10 and
96:9-10, presumes all kings are under the dominion of the Lord; rulers
represent all lands and peoples, for wisdom's invitation is universal. The
language of affection is used of the quest for wisdom in Wisdom of Solomon, to love, to seek (v. 1), to find (v. 2), to dwell (v. 4), to court (v. 12). Just
as the son or disciple in Proverbs must submit to discipline (*paideia*), so also
must kings/peoples of the earth in Wisdom 1:5, where *paideia* is translated
"discipline." To oppose the process of discipline is to "test [God]" (1:2),
which is the attitude of the wicked in 2:19. Wisdom literature usually gives

17

*King Solomon and the Queen of Sheba by Konrad Witz (1447). Solomon is the tenth
century B.C. Israelite king renowned for his wisdom.*

⁷For the spirit of the LORD fills the
world,
  is all-embracing, and knows
    whatever is said.
⁸Therefore those who utter wicked
    things will not go unnoticed,
  nor will chastising condemnation
    pass them by.
⁹For the devices of the wicked shall
    be scrutinized,
  and the sound of their words
    shall reach the LORD,
  for the chastisement of their
    transgressions;
¹⁰Because a jealous ear hearkens to
    everything,
  and discordant grumblings are
    not secret.

¹¹Therefore guard against profitless
    grumbling,
  and from calumny withhold your
    tongues;
For a stealthy utterance will not go
    unpunished,
  and a lying mouth destroys the
    soul.

¹²Do not court death by your erring
    way of life,
  nor draw to yourselves destruc-
    tion by the works of your
    hands.
¹³Because God did not make death, ▶
  nor does he rejoice in the destruc-
    tion of the living.

reasons for the conduct it teaches; one finds "because" and "for" throughout
the book (e.g., seven occurrences in 1:1-15 alone). The terms "justice,"
"goodness," "wisdom," "spirit of the LORD," "holy spirit," and "power,"
are chosen for their cumulative effect and in vv. 1-15 are virtually synony-
mous. Seeking wisdom is not a matter of the mind alone; one must be open
to discipline, must act justly, and revere God. The spirit as "all-embracing"
(1:7, literally: "holding all things together") was a Stoic expression for fiery
air that was thought to hold each thing together. The book applies that
function to God's spirit in 8:1.

  Older wisdom literature promised that those earnestly seeking wisdom
would gain life, which was understood in this-world terms as health, longevity, children, a suitable spouse, wealth, and reputation. Premature death
was the lot of the wicked; it symbolized failure to gain blessings. Wisdom
1:13-15 asserts something new: God did not make death the final dissolu-
tion of human beings, for the universe has a positive goal. The overarching
principle is stated in verse 14, "the creatures of the world are wholesome,"
i.e., all that is created preserves its being. The same verse conceives of "the
nether world" as a place of lethal power; that power does not extend to

▶ This symbol indicates a cross reference number in the *Catechism of the Catholic Church*. See
page 88 for number citations.

¹⁴For he fashioned all things that
 they might have being,
 and the creatures of the world
 are wholesome;
There is not a destructive drug among
 them
 nor any domain of Hades on
 earth,
¹⁵For righteousness is undying.

The Wicked Reject Immortality
and Righteousness Alike

¹⁶It was the wicked who with hands
 and words invited death,
 considered it a friend, and pined
 for it,
 and made a covenant with it,
Because they deserve to be allied
 with it.
2 ¹For, not thinking rightly, they said
 among themselves:
"Brief and troubled is our lifetime;
 there is no remedy for our dying,
 nor is anyone known to have come
 back from Hades.

²For by mere chance were we born,
 and hereafter we shall be as though
 we had not been;
Because the breath in our nostrils is
 smoke,
 and reason a spark from the beat-
 ing of our hearts,
³And when this is quenched, our
 body will be ashes
 and our spirit will be poured
 abroad like empty air.
⁴Even our name will be forgotten in
 time,
 and no one will recall our deeds.
So our life will pass away like the
 traces of a cloud,
 and will be dispersed like a mist
Pursued by the sun's rays
 and overpowered by its heat.
⁵For our lifetime is the passing of a
 shadow;
 and our dying cannot be deferred
 because it is fixed with a seal; and
 no one returns.
⁶Come, therefore, let us enjoy the
 good things that are here,

---

earth. Human beings die because of their mortality, but the power of death to end life permanently is ended.

1:16–2:24 The wicked and their plans

The righteous-wicked contrast (the "two worlds") is dramatized as an encounter between two groups about their beliefs and plans (2:1-9). How will the gang deal with a righteous individual who believes in the very things they reject (1:10-16)? They decide to test which way of life is valid, theirs or that of the righteous individual who boasts God is his father who will deliver his "son" from foes (1:17-18). They decide to kill him to see if God will do anything (v. 20). The answer will come in Wisdom 5. Wisdom 2 is framed by two verses (1:16 and 2:24) that highlight the words "death" and "possession" (Greek *meris*).

and make use of creation with
youthful zest.
⁷Let us have our fill of costly wine
and perfumes,
and let no springtime blossom
pass us by;
⁸let us crown ourselves with rose-
buds before they wither.
⁹Let no meadow be free from our
wantonness;
everywhere let us leave tokens
of our merriment,
for this is our portion, and this
our lot.
¹⁰Let us oppress the righteous poor;
let us neither spare the widow
nor revere the aged for hair grown
white with time.

¹¹But let our strength be our norm of
righteousness;
for weakness proves itself useless.

¹²Let us lie in wait for the righteous
one, because he is annoying
to us;
he opposes our actions,
Reproaches us for transgressions of
the law
and charges us with violations of
our training.
¹³He professes to have knowledge
of God
and styles himself a child of the
LORD.
¹⁴To us he is the censure of our
thoughts;

Each of the two ways has its adherents (i.e., those "in possession of" it). The wicked reveal their beliefs and behavior as well as those of the righteous individual (2:12-20). Their irreverence, pleasure seeking, and violence are an allusion to the opening scene in Proverbs 1:8-19. The wicked are said to consider death a friend and to make a covenant with it (Wis 1:16). "Covenant with death" borrows from Isaiah 28:15, where "death" is a metaphor for Egypt with whom some in Israel allied themselves instead of trusting in the Lord.

The father-son language in Wisdom 2 is borrowed from wisdom literature, in particular from Proverbs. Proverbs 3:12 teaches that, "whom the LORD loves he reproves, and he chastises the son he favors." Wisdom of Solomon regards the sufferings of the just "child of God" as divine reproof through which the son learns about divine governance. From Proverbs the author borrows the concept of "discipline" (Hebrew *mûsār*, Greek *paideia*) by which the teacher helps the disciple to become wise and mature; it can involve suffering. Also from Proverbs is the idea that the conduct of children honors or dishonors their parents (see Prov 10:1; 15:20; 17:21, 25; 19:13, 26; 23:22-26). Such is the sense of the accusation that the wicked have sinned against their "training" (*paideia*, 2:12). It is also possible, as some scholars have suggested, that the example of the loyal servant who is humiliated

merely to see him is a hardship
for us,
¹⁵Because his life is not like that of
others,
and different are his ways.
¹⁶He judges us debased;
he holds aloof from our paths as
from things impure.
He calls blest the destiny of the
righteous
and boasts that God is his Father.

¹⁷Let us see whether his words be
true;
let us find out what will happen
to him in the end.
¹⁸For if the righteous one is the son
of God, God will help him

and deliver him from the hand of
his foes.
¹⁹With violence and torture let us put
him to the test
that we may have proof of his
gentleness
and try his patience.
²⁰Let us condemn him to a shameful
death;
for according to his own words,
God will take care of him."

²¹These were their thoughts, but they
erred;
for their wickedness blinded
them,
²²And they did not know the hidden
counsels of God;

---

and then rescued by God (e.g., Joseph in Genesis 37–50 and the servant in Isaiah 53) has influenced Wisdom 2 and 5.

If "the devil" is indeed a reference to the devil, as most scholars hold, blaming the devil for death here is a striking innovation of the book. "Devil," however, is most probably not a good translation of Greek *diabolus*, which reflects Hebrew *satan*. "The satan" (with the article) referring to a particular figure occurs in two post-exilic texts (Job 1–2 and Zech 3:1-2) with a different meaning: "the satan" is an official of the heavenly court who scrutinizes human conduct and accuses them before God. In these passages, the Hebrew term *hassatan* means literally "the Adversary" or "Accuser." *Satan* (without the article) in 1 Chronicles 21:1 is disputed, but can mean "adversary" according to recent commentators. Such uncertainty makes attractive the view of St. Clement (*Epistle to the Corinthians* 3–4, A.D. 96), followed by some modern scholars, that Greek *diabolos* simply means "adversary" in Wisdom 2:24 and refers not to the snake who tempted the man and the woman in Genesis 3, but to Cain who murdered his brother Abel out of jealousy. In Wisdom 10:1-2, the author does not consider the sin of Adam as particularly grievous, but in 10:3-4 blames Cain for three instances of death: the death of Abel, Cain's own spiritual death of exile, and the death of almost the entire human race by flood. It is likely therefore that death entered the world through Cain's murder of Abel.

neither did they count on a
recompense for holiness
nor discern the innocent souls'
reward.
◄ ²³For God formed us to be imperishable;
the image of his own nature he
made us.
◄ ²⁴But by the envy of the devil, death
entered the world,
and they who are allied with him
experience it.

The Hidden Counsels of God

A. On Suffering

3 ¹The souls of the righteous are in
the hand of God,
and no torment shall touch them.
²They seemed, in the view of the
foolish, to be dead;
and their passing away was
thought an affliction
³and their going forth from us,
utter destruction.

3:1–4:20 The hidden meaning of the suffering of the just, the barrenness of the virtuous woman, and premature death

Instead of the proper conclusion to the story of the wicked versus the righteous individual begun in Wisdom 2, the author treats three classical problems of divine justice: the just who suffer (3:1-12), the virtuous woman who cannot bear children (3:13–4:6), and the premature death of a righteous person (4:7-20). The proper conclusion to the story will be told in Wisdom 5, deferring it until it then heightens interest in the problem of justice. Wisdom 3–4 can be considered an excursus, like those on the moderation of God toward sinners (11:15–12:27) and false worship (13:1–15:19).

3:1-12 The meaning of the suffering of the just

The torment of the just person depicted in Wisdom 2 raised the peren-nial question, why should "a child of the LORD" (2:13), a just person, suffer? This is the question of Job, and it is an abiding dilemma in biblical religion. This question is answered in the very first verse (3:1), they are in the hand of God, not in the "hand of [their] foes" (2:18). The following verses give supporting arguments: the righteous only *seemed* to be punished, but they are at peace (3:2-4); they were being tested (3:5-6; see Prov 3:11-12). Found worthy, they shall shine like the stars and rule like the angels with God (3:7-9; see Dan 12:1-3). That the righteous will rule Israel after their death is a corollary of their being with the angels in heaven, who were seen as servants of God. In contrast, the wicked are truly punished, have no hope, and their wives and children are accursed (3:10-12).

But they are in peace.
⁴For if to others, indeed, they seem
    punished,
    yet is their hope full of immor-
        tality;
⁵Chastised a little, they shall be
    greatly blessed,
    because God tried them
    and found them worthy of him-
        self.
⁶As gold in the furnace, he proved
    them,
    and as sacrificial offerings he
        took them to himself.
⁷In the time of their judgment they
    shall shine
    and dart about as sparks through
        stubble;
⁸They shall judge nations and rule
    over peoples,
    and the LORD shall be their King
        forever.
⁹Those who trust in him shall under-
    stand truth,
    and the faithful shall abide with
        him in love:
Because grace and mercy are with
    his holy ones,
    and his care is with the elect.

¹⁰But the wicked shall receive a
    punishment to match their
        thoughts,
    since they neglected righteous-
        ness and forsook the
        LORD.
¹¹For those who despise wisdom
    and instruction are doomed.
Vain is their hope, fruitless their
    labors,
    and worthless their works.
¹²Their wives are foolish and their
    children wicked,
    accursed their brood.

B. On Childlessness

¹³Yes, blessed is she who, childless
    and undefiled,
    never knew transgression of the
        marriage bed;
    for she shall bear fruit at the
        judgment of souls.
¹⁴So also the eunuch whose hand
    wrought no misdeed,
    who held no wicked thoughts
        against the LORD—
For he shall be given fidelity's choice
    reward

3:13–4:6 The virtuous woman who cannot bear children

As in the preceding section, this opens with a portrait of a type of person generally considered to be an argument *against* divine justice, a virtuous woman who was childless. Children were the means of living beyond death; the barren wives of Genesis (Sarah, Rebekah, Rachel) experienced a kind of resurrection when they had children. Not only such women, but virtuous eunuchs will also have their reward (3:14). The children of adulterers, on the other hand, will have no issue or die prematurely or in dishonor (3:16-19). They are a tree with shallow roots, vulnerable to strong winds, leaving behind no lasting fruit (4:3-6; see Psalm 1). The virtuous barren woman and eunuch, on the other hand, leave behind an immortal memory (4:1-2).

and a more gratifying heritage in
the LORD's temple.
¹⁵For the fruit of noble struggles is a
glorious one;
and unfailing is the root of understanding.
¹⁶But the children of adulterers will
remain without issue,
and the progeny of an unlawful
bed will disappear.
¹⁷For should they attain long life, they
will be held in no esteem,
and dishonored will their old age
be in the end;
¹⁸Should they die abruptly, they will
have no hope
nor comfort in the day of scrutiny;
¹⁹for dire is the end of the wicked
generation.

4 ¹Better is childlessness with virtue;
for immortal is the memory of
virtue,
acknowledged both by God and
human beings.
²When it is present people imitate it,
and they long for it when it is
gone;
Forever it marches crowned in
triumph,

victorious in unsullied deeds of
valor.
³But the numerous progeny of the
wicked shall be of no avail;
their spurious offshoots shall not
strike deep root
nor take firm hold.
⁴For even though their branches
flourish for a time,
they are unsteady and shall be
rocked by the wind
and, by the violence of the winds,
uprooted;
⁵Their twigs shall be broken off
untimely,
their fruit useless, unripe for
eating,
fit for nothing.
⁶For children born of lawless unions
give evidence of the wickedness
of their parents, when they
are examined.

C. On Early Death

⁷But the righteous one, though he die
early, shall be at rest.
⁸For the age that is honorable comes ▷
not with the passing of time,
nor can it be measured in terms
of years.

4:7-20 The premature death of a righteous person

A third obstacle to believing in a just God is the death of a "son" of this
God at a young age. If the fruit of righteousness is long life, how is God
just in this case? The author reinterprets old age as mature ripeness rather
than longevity as such (4:7-9) in view of immortality.

The example of Enoch (4:10-14) illustrates the teaching, though he is not
named, following the convention of wisdom literature. Enoch was the
seventh of the ten pre-Flood heroes in Genesis 5. Instead of dying, literally,
"[he] walked with God after the birth of Methuselah three hundred years,
and had other sons and daughters. Thus all the days of Enoch were three

⁹Rather, understanding passes for
gray hair,
and an unsullied life is the
attainment of old age.
¹⁰The one who pleased God was
loved,
living among sinners, was transported—
¹¹Snatched away, lest wickedness
pervert his mind
or deceit beguile his soul;
¹²For the witchery of paltry things
obscures what is right
and the whirl of desire transforms
the innocent mind.
¹³Having become perfect in a short
while,
he reached the fullness of a long
career;
¹⁴for his soul was pleasing to the
LORD,
therefore he sped him out of the
midst of wickedness.
But the people saw and did not
understand,
nor did they take that consider-
ation into account.

¹⁶Yes, the righteous one who has died
will condemn
the sinful who live;

And youth, swiftly completed, will
condemn
the many years of the unrighteous
who have grown old.
¹⁷For they will see the death of the
wise one
and will not understand what
the LORD intended,
or why he kept him safe.
¹⁸They will see, and hold him in
contempt;
but the LORD will laugh them to
scorn.
¹⁹And they shall afterward become
dishonored corpses
and an unceasing mockery among
the dead.
For he shall strike them down
speechless and prostrate
and rock them to their founda-
tions;
They shall be utterly laid waste
and shall be in grief
and their memory shall perish.

The Judgment of the Wicked

²⁰Fearful shall they come, at the
counting up of their sins,
and their lawless deeds shall
convict them to their face.

hundred sixty-five years. Enoch walked with God; then he was no more, because God took him" (Gen 5:22, 24, literal translation). He lived far fewer years than the other pre-Flood heroes, and the text does not explicitly say he died. Rather, he was "transported" (4:10), "snatched away" (4:11), because "he became perfect in a short while" (4:13); the latter phrase is an interpretation of Genesis 5:24, "Enoch walked with God."

The meaning of the death of the just person, however, is lost on the wicked (4:14c-19). Only at the final judgment will they understand. The nature of the judgment will be described in the next section.

5 ¹Then shall the righteous one with
great assurance confront
his oppressors who set at nought
his labors.
²Seeing this, the wicked shall be
shaken with dreadful fear,
and be amazed at the unexpected
salvation.
³They shall say among themselves,
rueful
and groaning through anguish
of spirit:

"This is the one whom once we held
as a laughingstock
and as a type for mockery,
⁴fools that we were!
His life we accounted madness,
and death dishonored.
⁵See how he is accounted among
the heavenly beings;
how his lot is with the holy
ones!

⁶We, then, have strayed from the way
of truth,
and the light of righteousness did
not shine for us,
and the sun did not rise for us.
⁷We were entangled in the thorns of
mischief and of ruin;
we journeyed through trackless
deserts,
but the way of the LORD we never
knew.
⁸What did our pride avail us?
What have wealth and its boast-
fulness afforded us?
⁹All of them passed like a shadow
and like a fleeting rumor;
¹⁰Like a ship traversing the heaving
water:
when it has passed, no trace can
be found,
no path of its keel in the waves.
¹¹Or like a bird flying through the
air;

5:1-23 The last judgment, confession of the wicked, and arming of the cosmos

The narrative of the gang's attack on the righteous individual, begun in Wisdom 2, is brought to its conclusion in Wisdom 5. The wicked presented their philosophy of life in their first speech (2:1-20) and retract it in their second speech (5:3-13). Both speeches are provoked by the righteous person, whom the wicked have failed to understand.

What is the scene? No details are given except that the wicked see the righteous person raised up from the dead. As noted in the Introduction, it is best interpreted as the judgment that precedes the new age when the righteous become rulers. Such judgment scenes are attested in classical biblical literature (e.g., Ps 82; Isa 41; 45:20-21; etc.). The scene that most closely resembles this one is Daniel 12:1-3; it too has those who have been killed in God's cause raised up, whereas their enemies are "in everlasting horror and disgrace." The view taken here is that this judgment precedes the final restoration; it is left vague because the author did not know the timetable, but only that those loyal to the Lord would rule in the new age.

no evidence of its course is to be
found—
But the fluid air, lashed by the beat-
ing of pinions,
and cleft by the rushing force
Of speeding wings, is traversed;
and afterward no mark of passage
can be found in it.
¹²Or as, when an arrow has been shot
at a mark,
the parted air straightway flows
together again
so that none discerns the way it
went—
¹³Even so, once born, we abruptly
came to nought
and held no sign of virtue to
display,
but were consumed in our
wickedness."

¹⁴Yes, the hope of the wicked is like
chaff borne by the wind,

and like fine, storm-driven snow;
Like smoke scattered by the wind,
and like the passing memory of
the nomad camping for a
single day.
¹⁵But the righteous live forever,
and in the LORD is their recompense,
and the thought of them is with
the Most High.
¹⁶Therefore shall they receive the
splendid crown,
the beautiful diadem, from the
hand of the LORD,
For he will shelter them with his
right hand,
and protect them with his arm.
¹⁷He shall take his zeal for armor
and arm creation to requite the
enemy,
¹⁸Shall put on righteousness for a
breastplate,
wear sure judgment for a helmet,

Thematically and rhetorically, Wisdom 5 develops 4:7-20, for the series of initial verbs in 4:17–5:1 reach their climax in 5:1: "they [the wicked] see," "see," "shall afterward become," "shall be," "shall be," "shall they come," "the just one" will "confront." As in Wisdom 2, the just person is silent, the mere sight of the risen one provokes self-condemnation on the part of the attackers. Their confession in 5:5, "See how he is accounted among the heavenly beings" (literally "sons of God") evokes Matthew 27:54 and Mark 15:39, where the wonders accompanying the death of Jesus lead the centurion to cry out, "Truly this man was the Son of God!" The wicked, citizens of this world only, did not *know* until they saw the just one raised from the dead; now they understand "justice is undying" (Wis 1:15). They are shamed, in the biblical sense, i.e., what they relied on is shown to be illusory. The real world, normally hidden, becomes visible when the just person trusts in God and is raised from the dead.

The confession of the wicked in 5:6-13 is a vivid and even poignant description of the life they believe ends definitively with death. The point is made largely through variations on one image, "way": we strayed from the way (5:6-8); our own fleeting way is like a shadow, a word (5:9), the fleet-

[19]Shall take invincible holiness for a shield,
[20]and sharpen his sudden anger for a sword.
The universe will war with him against the foolhardy;
[21]Well-aimed bolts of lightning will go forth
and from the clouds will leap to the mark as from a well-drawn bow;[a]
[22]and as from a sling, wrathful hailstones shall be hurled.
The waters of the sea will be enraged
and flooding rivers will overwhelm them;
[23]A mighty wind will confront them and winnow them like a tempest;
Thus lawlessness will lay waste the whole earth
and evildoing overturn the thrones of the mighty.

Exhortation to Seek Wisdom

6 [1]Hear, therefore, kings, and understand;
learn, you magistrates of the earth's expanse!

ing wake of a ship (5:10), the air unaffected by a bird's flight (5:11), the course of an arrow (5:12). Their conclusion is in 5:13: our wickedness is the cause of our demise. The comparisons are inspired perhaps by the poem on the "way" in Proverbs 30:18-20. The author confirms the self-judgment of the wicked, nicely picking up the images of air and water (Wis 5:14).

What is the divine protection that means life for the just? The final part of Wisdom 5 (vv. 16-23) describes the arming of the Storm God and the employment of the storm weapons against that which rebels against the justice implanted in the world. The Scriptures often portray the Lord as a Storm God (e.g., Exod 15:1-18; Judg 5; Ps 29). The imagery is even older than the biblical portraits; the Storm God used thunder, lightning, wind, and rain against his enemies to gain kingship over the universe. Wisdom 5:17 draws on Isaiah 59:17, "He put on justice as his breastplate, / victory as a helmet on his head; / He clothed himself with garments of vengeance, / wrapped himself in a mantle of zeal." The author gives a new emphasis, "[the Lord] shall arm creation to requite the enemy," i.e., creation itself will fight against injustice. The arming of creation will be particularly clear in part 3 in which the natural phenomena of the seven plagues of the exodus are used to punish the wicked (the Egyptians) and benefit the children of God (Israel).

6:1-21 Seek wisdom and avoid judgment

The author returns to the authoritative warnings and exhortations to kings that began part 1 (Wis 1:1-15), bringing the structure of this part to its conclusion. Wisdom 1:1-15 warned the kings they are being judged by God

The Storm God used lightning, thunder, wind and rain against his enemies to gain kingship over the universe (Wisdom 5:20-23).

²Give ear, you who have power over
multitudes
and lord it over throngs of peoples!
³Because authority was given you by
the Lord
and sovereignty by the Most High,
who shall probe your works and
scrutinize your counsels!
⁴Because, though you were ministers
of his kingdom, you did not
judge rightly,
and did not keep the law,
nor walk according to the will of
God,
⁵Terribly and swiftly he shall come
against you,
because severe judgment awaits
the exalted—
⁶For the lowly may be pardoned out
of mercy
but the mighty shall be mightily
put to the test.
⁷For the Ruler of all shows no par-
tiality,
nor does he fear greatness,

Because he himself made the great
as well as the small,
and provides for all alike;
⁸but for those in power a rigorous
scrutiny impends.

⁹To you, therefore, O princes, are my
words addressed
that you may learn wisdom and
that you may not fall
away.
¹⁰For those who keep the holy
precepts hallowed will be
found holy,
and those learned in them will
have ready a response.
¹¹Desire therefore my words;
long for them and you will be
instructed.
¹²Resplendent and unfading is
Wisdom,
and she is readily perceived by
those who love her,
and found by those who seek
her.

whose spirit fills the world and scrutinizes their performance; 6:1-21 again
reminds them they rule only as servants of God who will judge them im-
partially (vv. 1-8). Wisdom 6:9-11 marks the transition from warning against
lawless behavior to positive seeking of wisdom. Borrowing Proverbs' per-
sonification of wisdom and exhortation to seek her (Prov 1–9), the author
retains Proverbs' paradox that one must earnestly *seek* wisdom so that God
can *bestow* it as a gift. The relationship of the individual ideal king to wisdom is portrayed in Wisdom 6:12-16 with the language of love. The relationship culminates in wisdom's bestowing true sovereignty upon her
faithful and loving friend ("the desire for Wisdom leads to a kingdom").
The section that concludes part 1 also introduces part 2 by its introduction
of wisdom as lover who is to be courted.

In biblical categories, the kings represent the nations; in addressing
kings, the author addresses all nations and every person, asserting that
each is under the one Lord. In Wisdom 6:4, "the law" is not the Mosaic law
as such but natural principles of justice, knowledge of which could be ex-

30

¹³She hastens to make herself known
    to those who desire her;
¹⁴one who watches for her at dawn
        will not be disappointed,
    for she will be found sitting at
        the gate.
¹⁵For setting your heart on her is the
        perfection of prudence,
    and whoever keeps vigil for her
        is quickly free from care;
¹⁶Because she makes her rounds,
        seeking those worthy of her,
    and graciously appears to them
        on the way,
    and goes to meet them with full
        attention.

¹⁷For the first step toward Wisdom
        is an earnest desire for disci-
        pline;
¹⁸then, care for discipline is love
        of her;
    love means the keeping of her
        laws;
To observe her laws is the basis for
        incorruptibility;
¹⁹and incorruptibility makes one
        close to God;
²⁰thus the desire for Wisdom leads
        to a kingdom.
²¹If, then, you find pleasure in throne
        and scepter, you princes of
        peoples,

---

pected from every ruler and every person. The section is brought to its conclusion in Wisdom 6:17-20 by a rhetorical figure called a chain syllogism or *sorites* in which each proposition leads to another and the whole series ends with a surprise declaration ("desire for discipline," leads to "love," love means "keeping of her laws," which in turn is the "basis for incorruptibility," bringing one "close to God," in other words to the "kingdom"). To paraphrase: if you want to retain your ability to rule, pursue wisdom and you will attain the fullness of rule.

Part 1 has emphasized again and again that the world is ruled by the spirit and wisdom of God, not by the kings that one sees in daily life. There is thus operative in the world a *hidden* authority; unknown to most people, it becomes visible especially when a "child [or servant] of God" trusts completely in God. Can we know more about this mysterious power in the universe, and can we encounter it to enrich our lives? That question will be answered in the next section of the book.

WISDOM AND THE WAY TO IT

6:22–10:21

Part 1 warned kings to recognize that they owe obeisance to the Lord who rules the world through power, spirit, and wisdom (1:1-15 and 6:1-21). In 6:1-21, wisdom becomes the preferred term for divine rule (6:9, 12, 20,

honor Wisdom, that you may
reign as kings forever.

II. Praise of Wisdom by Solomon

Introduction

²²Now what wisdom is, and how she
came to be I shall proclaim;
and I shall conceal no secrets
from you,
But from the very beginning I shall
search out

and bring to light knowledge of
her;
I shall not diverge from the truth.
²³Neither shall I admit consuming
jealousy to my company,
because that can have no fellow-
ship with Wisdom.
²⁴A multitude of the wise is the
safety of the world,
and a prudent king, the stability
of the people;
²⁵so take instruction from my
words, to your profit.

21). In part 2 the wise king (Solomon, not named according to the typifying convention of wisdom literature), speaking in the first person, instructs the kings of the world. The wise king emphasizes the common humanity shared with all people and gives his secret: his ardent and unremitting quest of wisdom since childhood. The quest is something *all* can embark on and is not limited to one nation. Wisdom has guided the whole course of human history by raising up wise individuals in every generation (Wis 10). Wisdom 10 is the link between parts 2 and 3 (God's guidance of Israel in Egypt), for the eighth in the line of wisdom heroes is Moses, the leader of the exodus that will be the center of attention in part 3 (10:16).

This section has two parts. Seven passages (6:22–8:21) in chiastic order describe Solomon's quest; this is followed by his great prayer for wisdom (Wis 9) and eight episodes about wisdom heroes (Wis 10).

6:22-25 Introduction

The verses serve as a transition from part 1 and a preview of part 2. Up to this point in the book, kings (representing the Gentile nations) have been warned to seek wisdom or incur divine wrath in the coming judgment (Wis 1:1-15; 6:1-21). Now one king addresses the whole world ("I" in 6:22) with an authority gained from seeking and finding wisdom. This king will describe his own quest and gift of wisdom (7:1–8:2a; 8:2–9:18), what wisdom is (7:22b–8:1), and how she rules the world (ch. 10). In the Egyptian culture of the day, mystery cults had secret lore known only to the initiates. Following the example of Woman Wisdom in Proverbs (see Prov 1:20-21 and 8:1-3),

Solomon Is Like All Others

7 ¹I too am a mortal, the same as all
the rest,
and a descendant of the first one
formed of earth.
And in my mother's womb I was
molded into flesh
²in a ten-month period—body
and blood,
from the seed of a man, and the
pleasure that accompanies
marriage.

³And I too, when born, inhaled the
common air,
and fell upon the kindred earth;
wailing, I uttered that first sound
common to all.
⁴In swaddling clothes and with
constant care I was nurtured.
⁵For no king has any different origin
or birth;
⁶one is the entry into life for all,
and in one same way they leave
it.

---

the king speaks *openly* to all (6:22b). The Jewish philosopher Philo also attacked secretive pagan mysteries, citing Plato that "jealousy" (6:23) is incompatible with wisdom's freehanded pouring forth knowledge (Philo, *Quod omnis probus liber sit* 13–14). Moreover, "jealousy" provoked the adversary to bring death into the world (Wis 2:24). Going beyond the view of wisdom as enriching only individuals, 6:24 says that wise people benefit the world and a wise king benefits his people (cf. Prov 29:4); Wisdom 10 will illustrate this assertion.

The King's Quest for Wisdom and Celebration of Her Virtues (7:1–8:21)

For a detailed outline of this lengthy speech, see the Introduction. Wisdom is not a doctrine one human being can impart to another. Rather, it is a gift given by God to those who earnestly seek it. The king's "teaching" is therefore the story of his own strivings after it and of God's granting it, as well as a description of wisdom in herself (7:22b–8:1).

7:1-6 The origin of the king is like any other human

The beginning and end of the section are marked by the words "the same" / "one same way" in verses 1 and 6. The king is wise not because of his kingship but because of his lifelong quest for wisdom. The Gentile kings were told to seek wisdom (1:1-15 and 6:1-21) and this king has done just that. Kingship, which in the ancient East and especially in Egypt was more than a human state, is here demystified. "Ten month period" is a Greek way of reckoning pregnancy; Hebrew tradition reckoned it as nine months (2 Macc 7:27).

Solomon Prayed and Wisdom and Riches Came to Him

⁷Therefore I prayed, and prudence
was given me;
I pleaded and the spirit of
Wisdom came to me.
⁸I preferred her to scepter and throne,
And deemed riches nothing in comparison with her,
⁹nor did I liken any priceless gem
to her;
Because all gold, in view of her, is a
bit of sand,
and before her, silver is to be
accounted mire.
¹⁰Beyond health and beauty I loved
her,
And I chose to have her rather than
the light,
because her radiance never ceases.
¹¹Yet all good things together came
to me with her,
and countless riches at her hands;
¹²I rejoiced in them all, because
Wisdom is their leader,
though I had not known that she
is their mother.

Solomon Prays for Help to Speak Worthily of Wisdom

¹³Sincerely I learned about her, and
ungrudgingly do I share—
her riches I do not hide away;
¹⁴For she is an unfailing treasure;

7:7-12 So I prayed for wisdom

Given that wisdom is a gift, it is not surprising that the king now tells us of his constant prayer for it and *preference* of it over gold and silver. The text alludes to the famous dream in 1 Kings 3 where God, pleased that Solomon preferred wisdom to long life or riches, or for the life of his enemies, gave him "a heart so wise and discerning that there has never been anyone like you until now, nor after you will there be anyone to equal you" (1 Kgs 3:11-13). Preferring wisdom over gold and silver is a theme from Proverbs, e.g., Proverbs 8:10-11: "Take my instruction instead of silver, and knowledge rather than choice gold. / [For wisdom is better than corals, and no treasure can compare with her.]" "Wisdom is their leader , though I had not known that she is their mother." (7:12). Proverbs portrayed wisdom as a bride and lover, but not as a mother. Like a mother, wisdom brings to birth human possibilities for happiness.

7:13-22a Gift of knowledge of God to Solomon

The section is marked off by "hide away" in verse 13b and "hidden" in verse 21a. The king is about to expound what wisdom is (7:22b–8:1) and prepares for that auspicious moment by a prayer, "God grant I speak suitably" (v. 15). The king said, "I shall conceal no secrets from you" in the introduction (6:22), for no one can hide what is gratuitously given by the

those who gain this treasure win
    the friendship of God,
being commended by the gifts
    that come from her disci-
    pline.
¹⁵Now God grant I speak suitably
    and value these endowments at
    their worth:
For he is the guide of Wisdom
    and the director of the wise.
◄   ¹⁶For both we and our words are in
    his hand,
as well as all prudence and
    knowledge of crafts.
◄   ¹⁷For he gave me sound knowledge
    of what exists,
that I might know the structure
    of the universe and the
    force of its elements,
¹⁸The beginning and the end and
    the midpoint of times,

the changes in the sun's course
    and the variations of the
    seasons,
¹⁹Cycles of years, positions of stars,
    ²⁰natures of living things, tempers
    of beasts,
Powers of the winds and thoughts
    of human beings,
uses of plants and virtues of
    roots—
²¹Whatever is hidden or plain I
    learned,
    ²²for Wisdom, the artisan of all,
    taught me.

**Nature and Incomparable
Dignity of Wisdom**

For in her is a spirit
    intelligent, holy, unique,
Manifold, subtle, agile,
    clear, unstained, certain,

---

generous God (7:13). The author is careful not to make wisdom an entity separate from God. Rather, it is a divine gift enabling people to have a relationship with God (7:14-15). Verses 15-16 emphasize the close relationship of wisdom to God: "[God] is the guide of Wisdom and the director of the wise." Part 3 will no longer refer to wisdom as a subject who acts, replacing it with God who acts for Israel.

In both Hellenistic philosophy and traditional Near Eastern religions, wisdom included the knowledge of what moderns call science. The philosopher Aristotle (384–322 B.C.) wrote both philosophical and scientific treatises; Stoicism was a cosmology as well as a philosophy; and Solomon "spoke of plants, from the cedar on Lebanon to the hyssop growing out of the wall, and he spoke about beasts, birds, reptiles, and fishes" (1 Kgs 5:13, other versions 4:33). Wisdom makes people careful and discerning observers of the universe God made.

7:22b–8:1 Praise of wisdom, its nature, origin, action, and attributes

This section is the center and core of the king's speech, for it describes what the introduction promised, "what Wisdom is, and how she came to

Never harmful, loving the good,
  keen,
²³unhampered, beneficent, kindly,
Firm, secure, tranquil,
  all-powerful, all-seeing,
And pervading all spirits,
  though they be intelligent, pure
    and very subtle.
²⁴For Wisdom is mobile beyond all
  motion,
  and she penetrates and pervades
    all things by reason of her
    purity.
²⁵For she is a breath of the might of
  God
  and a pure emanation of the
    glory of the Almighty;
  therefore nothing defiled can
    enter into her.

²⁶For she is the reflection of eternal
  light,
  the spotless mirror of the power
    of God,
  the image of his goodness.
²⁷Although she is one, she can do all
  things,
  and she renews everything while
    herself perduring;
Passing into holy souls from age to
  age,
  she produces friends of God and
    prophets.
²⁸For God loves nothing so much as
  the one who dwells with
  Wisdom.
²⁹For she is fairer than the sun
  and surpasses every constellation
    of the stars.

---

be" (6:22). The first section (7:22b-23) is a list of attributes of wisdom, using the sacred numbers three times seven to yield twenty-one attributes. The terminology and the genre are Greek. Hellenistic religions employed such lists, sometimes called aretalogies (literally, accounts of virtue), to gain adherents. Aretalogies were especially associated with Isis, originally an Egyptian goddess, who became popular in Greek and Roman religions as a model sister, wife, and great mother. The terms for wisdom are influenced by the Stoic world-spirit thought to be immanent in the universe. It permeates and pervades (the same words as Wis 6:24) all things, and communicates virtue to intelligent creatures.

The twenty-one attributes make their impression cumulatively rather than singly. The first cluster of seven underscores the intelligence, transcendence, and mobility of wisdom, the second cluster underscores her purity, benefits to humans, and reliability, and the third her subtlety and ability to enter within all things. These attributes go considerably beyond the portraits of wisdom in Proverbs 8 and Sirach 24, for they transpose wisdom into spirit and make her able to *animate* natural phenomena as well as human beings.

Wisdom 7:25-26 is a memorable five-fold metaphor for wisdom, each part of which relates wisdom to an aspect of God: "aura" (better: exhalation, breath) of the power of God, "effusion" or outflowing of the divine glory,

Compared to light, she is found more
radiant;
[30]though night supplants light,
wickedness does not prevail over
Wisdom.

8 [1]Indeed, she spans the world from
end to end mightily
and governs all things well.

Wisdom, the Source of Blessings

[2]Her I loved and sought after from
my youth;
I sought to take her for my bride
and was enamored of her beauty.

[3]She adds to nobility the splendor of
companionship with God;
even the Ruler of all loved her.
[4]For she leads into the understanding
of God,
and chooses his works.
[5]If riches are desirable in life,
what is richer than Wisdom, who
produces all things?
[6]And if prudence is at work,
who in the world is a better
artisan than she?
[7]Or if one loves righteousness,
whose works are virtues,

"refulgence" or reflection of eternal light, a "spotless mirror" of the divine energy, "the image" of divine goodness. The language is daring especially for an author writing in the biblical tradition. Even Philo does not use such terms as "effusion" or "reflection" for the origin of the Divine Logos. Wisdom 7:27-28 speaks of wisdom's governance of the world. Wisdom herself remains unaffected as she affects others, which is a sure sign of transcendence and superiority.

Beyond assuring the cohesion and order of the universe, wisdom enters into humans, becoming the principle of their moral and religious life. She enters into certain people in every generation. Wisdom 7:27cd views the divine call as wisdom entering a person, "passing into holy souls from age to age, she produces friends of God and prophets." Luke 7:35, "wisdom is vindicated by all her children," seems to draw on this concept of vocation to portray Jesus as an emissary of wisdom. Wisdom 10 describes wisdom-inspired heroes in the book of Genesis. Wisdom has her own people in every age. Sirach 44–50 similarly viewed history as a series of spirit-inspired individuals.

Again, like Ben Sira (Sir 16:26-28; 42:15–43:33), the author credits wisdom with the operation of the universe (Wis 7:29-30). "Reaches from end to end" (8:1) draws on Stoic cosmology, in which the movement of the world was caused by a continuous outward-inward movement of air from the center to the outermost pole.

8:2-9 Solomon will marry wisdom who lives with God

The section balances 7:13-22a by repeating its themes of wealth, knowledge, wisdom's relationship to God (8:3), and virtues including "science"

She teaches moderation and prudence,
  righteousness and fortitude,
  and nothing in life is more use-
  ful than these.
[8]Or again, if one yearns for wide
experience,
  she knows the things of old, and
  infers the things to come.
She understands the turns of phrases
  and the solutions of riddles;
  signs and wonders she knows in
  advance
and the outcome of times and
ages.

Wisdom as Solomon's Counselor and Comfort

[9]So I determined to take her to live
with me,
  knowing that she would be my
  counselor while all was
  well,
  and my comfort in care and grief.
[10]Because of her I have glory among
the multitudes,
  and esteem from the elders, though
  I am but a youth.
[11]I shall become keen in judgment,
  and shall be a marvel before
  rulers.

(8:8 = 7:17-22a). It speaks of them from a different perspective, however—that of the ardent suitor of Woman Wisdom. Her gifts are personal and given directly to her lover, the king. The beginning and end of this section is marked by the inclusion of "to take her" in both verse 2 and verse 9. The portrayal of Woman Wisdom as a beautiful woman seeking suitors (8:2) is traditional (e.g., Prov 1:20-33; 7:4; ch. 8; 9:1-6, 11; Sir 14:23-25; 15:2-6; 51:13-22).

Paradoxically, seeking *one* thing (wisdom) means that *all* things will be given (cf. Matt 6:33 and parallels.). Her closeness to God makes her lead into (Wis 8:4, Greek: *mustis*) divine knowledge. The Greek term was used in the mystery religions for the highest level of knowledge. Encompassing all knowledge, Wisdom can give all else, for knowledge is the central virtue in Wisdom of Solomon. Among wisdom's gifts are "moderation and prudence, justice and fortitude" (8:7c), which is the first mention in Scripture of the four cardinal virtues. The cardinal virtues (from Latin *cardo*, "hinge") occur in Greek philosophical debate from the time of Plato and Aristotle as a means of unifying the virtuous life. The author is integrating the Greek ideal with the biblical tradition. The cardinal virtues became a staple of Christian tradition, being later discussed by St. Ambrose, St. Augustine, and St. Thomas Aquinas.

8:10-16 Thoughts of the young Solomon

The section balances section 7:7-12 in that both sections allude to 1 Kings 3 and Proverbs 8, which tell of Solomon being granted wisdom, his prefer-

¹²They will wait while I am silent
 and listen when I speak;
 and when I shall speak the more,
 they will put their hands upon
 their mouths.
¹³Because of her I shall have immortality
 and leave to those after me an
 everlasting memory.
¹⁴I shall govern peoples, and nations
 will be my subjects—
 ¹⁵tyrannical princes, hearing of me,
 will be afraid;
 in the assembly I shall appear
 noble, and in war coura-
 geous.
¹⁶Entering my house, I shall take my
 repose beside her;

For association with her involves no
 bitterness
 and living with her no grief,
 but rather joy and gladness.

Wisdom is a Gift of God

¹⁷Reflecting on these things,
 and considering in my heart
That immortality lies in kinship with
 Wisdom,
 ¹⁸great delight in love of her,
 and unfailing riches in the works
 of her hands;
And that in associating with her
 there is prudence,
 and fair renown in sharing her
 discourses,

ence for wisdom over gold and silver, and the necessity of wisdom for governing. Common to the two sections in Wisdom of Solomon is the mention of by-products of the quest for wisdom, riches (7:7-12), and fame (8:10-16). Fame in the latter passage has two aspects: prestige in this life (8:10-12, 14-15) and immortality in the next (8:13). Both aspects are characteristics of Solomon in 1 Kings 3–11. In 1 Kings 3:6-9, the young Solomon asked for wisdom to govern like his father David. Solomon also won "immortality" in the sense of enduring fame by his judgment on the true mother of the child (1 Kgs 3:28) and by his vast knowledge (1 Kgs 4:34; 10:6-10).

8:17-21 Young Solomon will ask for wisdom

The section, marked off by "heart" in verses 17b and 21d, balances 7:1-6. Both sections underscore the humanity the king shares with all people and that one needs wisdom to bring one's humanity to perfection. In both sections, the realization leads to prayer, in 7:7 and in Wisdom 9.

Wisdom 8:19-20, literally, "I was a well-favored child, / having a noble soul fall to my lot, / or rather, being noble, I entered an undefiled body," show an awareness of the Greek philosophical idea of the preexistence of souls. The view is classically stated in the myth of Er in Book 10 of Plato's *Republic*, "Now is the beginning of another cycle of mortal generation. . . . Let him to whom falls the first lot first select a life to which he shall leave

I went about seeking to take her
for my own.
¹⁹Now, I was a well-favored child,
and I came by a noble nature;
²⁰or rather, being noble, I attained
an unblemished body.
²¹And knowing that I could not
otherwise possess her unless
God gave it—
and this, too, was prudence, to
know whose gift she is—
I went to the LORD and besought him,
and said with all my heart:

Solomon's Prayer

9 ¹God of my ancestors, Lord of mercy,
you who have made all things by
your word
²And in your wisdom have established humankind
to rule the creatures produced by
you,
³And to govern the world in holiness
and righteousness,
and to render judgment in integrity of heart:

---

of necessity." The pre-existence of souls did not play a major role in Wisdom of Solomon. Wisdom 9:15 similarly has Greek vocabulary, "For the corruptible body burdens the soul."

The Prayer of the King for Wisdom (9:1-18)

The king's prayer is the center of the section and indeed of the entire book. In chapters 7–8, the king explained that his entire life has been dedicated to seeking wisdom, and now recalls how he acquired wisdom through prayer. Chapters 7–8 pointed to the prayer at their beginning (7:7) and end (8:21). Part 1 (Wis 1–6) demonstrated the hidden energy of the world (wisdom), warning kings they risk punishment if they overlook it. Part 3 (Wis 11–19) will show how that wisdom-energy benefited Israel and punished their enemy. Wisdom 9 shows the ideal king uttering a model prayer for wisdom. The prayer thus bridges parts 1 and 3. By its reference to creation ("you who have *made* all things . . . have *established* [humankind]," 9:1-2), it refers to part 1, and by its reference to salvation ("and people learned what pleases you, and were *saved* by Wisdom," 9:18), it alludes to part 3. The prayer itself is divided into three parts by its topics: verses 1-6 focus upon human beings, verses 7-12 the king, verses 13-18 human beings.

9:1-6 As a limited human being I stand in need of your wisdom

The first part builds on venerable texts about Solomon the wise king and wisdom as an attendant at God's throne. At the very beginning of his reign, Solomon confessed his inadequacy, "I am a mere youth, not knowing at all how to act" (1 Kgs 3:7; cf. Wis 9:5-6), and asked for "a listening heart

⁴Give me Wisdom, the consort at
    your throne,
    and do not reject me from among
        your children;
⁵For I am your servant, the child of
    your maidservant,
    a man weak and short-lived
    and lacking in comprehension of
        judgment and of laws.
⁶Indeed, though one be perfect among
    mortals,
    if Wisdom, who comes from you,
    be lacking,
    that one will count for nothing.

⁷You have chosen me king over your
    people
    and magistrate over your sons
    and daughters.
⁸You have bid me build a temple on
    your holy mountain
    and an altar in the city that is your
    dwelling place,
    a copy of the holy tabernacle
    which you had established
    from of old.
⁹Now with you is Wisdom, who
    knows your works

---

to judge [govern] your people" (1 Kgs 3:9; cf. Wis 9:4). The royal prayer in Wisdom 9, however, is broader than its prototype in 1 Kings 3. It harks back to Genesis and Exodus by the use of the divine name, "God of my ancestors" (Wis 9:1; "the God of Abraham, Isaac, and Jacob," see Gen 28:13 and Exod 3:6) and to Genesis 1 by "you who have made all things by your word" (Wis 9:1) and the assignment to humans of governing the world (Wis 9:2-3; cf. Gen 1:26-28). "Wisdom, the consort at your throne" (Wis 9:4) echoes Prov 8:30, "then was I beside him as artisan."

The first section of Solomon's prayer (9:1-6) is concerned with Solomon as a human being rather than as king. It nonetheless presupposes that all humans, not kings alone, have a vocation to govern the world. For this reason, the warnings to kings in Wisdom 1:1-15 and 6:1-21 include *all* human beings, not kings only. Despite its occasional denunciations, Wisdom of Solomon has an extremely high evaluation of humans. Its high assessment of humans and their vocation in fact accounts for the severity of the criticism.

The book considers the gift of wisdom a *complement* to native human excellence, not a replacement for it. Though the book employs the fashionable body-soul language of Middle Platonism (e.g., 8:19-20; 9:15), its underlying view of the human person is biblical, i.e., an animated body. The body is regarded as good.

9:7-12 Send me wisdom to build you a house and help me govern

The second part of the prayer is concerned with Solomon *as king*. The account of Solomon's reign in 1 Kings 1–11 tells of the "wisdom" of Solomon

and was present when you made
the world;
Who understands what is pleasing
in your eyes
and what is conformable with
your commands.
¹⁰Send her forth from your holy
heavens
and from your glorious throne
dispatch her
That she may be with me and work
with me,
that I may know what is pleasing
to you.
¹¹For she knows and understands all
things,

and will guide me prudently in
my affairs
and safeguard me by her glory;
¹²Thus my deeds will be acceptable,
and I will judge your people
justly
and be worthy of my father's
throne.

¹³For who knows God's counsel,
or who can conceive what the
Lord intends?
¹⁴For the deliberations of mortals are
timid,
and uncertain our plans.
¹⁵For the corruptible body burdens
the soul

---

in governing well—deciding, organizing, and building. Almost forty percent of the account in 1 Kings is devoted to his planning, building, and dedicating the temple. It is not, therefore, surprising that Wisdom 9:7-10 is devoted to constructing the temple. The temple is the symbol of a transcendent heavenly reality given from heaven. In biblical thought, realities existing in heaven could be copied on earth so that their virtues affected human beings. In Exodus 25:9, God tells Moses to make the tabernacle and all its furniture, exactly "according to all that I show you regarding the pattern" and rabbinic tradition included the torah among those things descended from heaven. The Platonic tradition also assumed a correspondence between heavenly reality and earthly copy. In Solomon's prayer, the temple is a symbol of the wisdom from heaven that enables humans on earth to do what is pleasing to God (9:10).

9:13-18 Humans require wisdom to be saved

The last section returns to the theme of humans as such. It stresses the limits of human knowing. For humans to know and do the divine will, God must take the first step and send wisdom. Revelation is absolutely necessary for humans to be pleasing to God (9:18). The Platonic echo in 9:15, "the corruptible body burdens the soul," is less a statement about the constitution of humans than a psychological statement about ill-informed desire. Wisdom 4:12 is similar: "For the witchery of paltry things obscures what

and the earthly tent weighs down
the mind with its many
concerns.
¹⁶Scarcely can we guess the things
on earth,
and only with difficulty grasp
what is at hand;
but things in heaven, who can
search them out?

¹⁷Or who can know your counsel,
unless you give Wisdom
and send your holy spirit from
on high?
¹⁸Thus were the paths of those on
earth made straight,
and people learned what pleases
you,
and were saved by Wisdom.

is right, and the whirl of desire transforms the innocent mind." The human race, in short, requires divine intervention if it is to do what is pleasing to God. This conviction provokes the last assertion of the king, people "were *saved* by Wisdom" (9:18; emphasis added). As the prayer began by addressing God as creator, it ends by addressing God as savior. The mention of salvation introduces the next chapter, on the seven plus one wisdom heroes who saved the world in their generations.

In Every Age Wisdom Forms Friends of God and Prophets (10:1-21)

Wisdom 10 is the story of the human race to the formation of Israel ("the holy people," 10:15) told as a series of personalities of the torah who were guided by wisdom. The eight contrasts are sketched with great variety: Adam/his fall (vv. 1-2a), Abel/Cain (vv. 2b-3), Noah/the flooded earth (v. 4), Abraham/the wicked nations (v. 5), Lot/the wicked (vv. 6-9), Jacob/ Esau and Laban (vv. 10-12), Joseph/Potiphar's wife (vv. 13-14), and Moses/ Pharaoh and enemies (vv. 15-21). Moses, the eighth, stands outside the series, for with him there begins something new, the story of Israel as the child of God. The feminine pronoun for "wisdom" (Greek *hautē*) begins verses 1, 5, 6, 10, 13, 15. The technique can be called midrashic, for scriptural data are elaborated through story to bring out their meaning for a contemporary audience. Sirach 44–50 also regards history as a succession of wisdom-inspired individuals.

Wisdom 10 looks backward and forward in the book. With its seven just individuals delivered by wisdom (vv. 6, 9, 13, 15), it illustrates the deliverance of the prototypical just individual in Wisdom 2 (see esp. 2:18). Wisdom 2 is schematic and abstract and Wisdom 10 is concrete and historical. Wisdom 10 also illustrates Wisdom 7:27, for Wisdom passes "into holy souls from age to age, she produces friends of God and prophets." Finally, Wisdom 10 looks forward in that the eighth wisdom hero, Moses, points to part 3 where Israel, child of God, is protected in the exodus.

Wisdom Preserves Her Followers

10 ¹She preserved the first-formed
father of the world
when he alone had been created;
And she raised him up from his fall,
²and gave him power to rule all
things.
³But when an unrighteous man with-
drew from her in his anger,
he perished through his fratri-
cidal wrath.
⁴When on his account the earth was
flooded, Wisdom again
saved it,
piloting the righteous man on
frailest wood.
⁵She, when the nations were sunk in
universal wickedness,
knew the righteous man, kept
him blameless before God,
and preserved him resolute
against pity for his child.

⁶She rescued a righteous man from
among the wicked who were
being destroyed,
when he fled as fire descended
upon the Pentapolis—
⁷Where as a testimony to its wickedness,
even yet there remain a smoking
desert,
Plants bearing fruit that never ripens,
and the tomb of a disbelieving
soul, a standing pillar of
salt.
⁸For those who forsook Wisdom
not only were deprived of
knowledge of the good,
But also left the world a memorial
of their folly,

10:1-4 Adam, Cain, and Noah

These three individuals are from Genesis 1–11, the time before Abraham. Adam is the first human being and the first sinner. Hence, wisdom "pre-served" him and "raised him up" from his transgression (10:1, NAB "fall") and enabled him to exercise the ruling function assigned to human beings in Genesis 1:26-28. Because he murdered his brother Abel (Gen 4:1-16), wisdom destroys Cain, prefiguring the divine destruction of the Canaanites and Egyptians in part 3. Wisdom sees to it that the just Noah saved the earth flooded in punishment for Cain's offense.

10:5-9 Abraham and Lot

Abraham is remembered for his faith, most memorably expressed in his sacrifice of his son Isaac (Gen 22). By this time in Judaism, Abraham's pa-ternal feelings had become a subject of much reflection; wisdom is credited with ensuring that such feelings did not prevent him from carrying out the divine will. Contrary to the less-than-admirable picture of Lot in Genesis 13–19, Lot here is described as a righteous man in contrast to his neighbors and his disbelieving wife. Their strange fates, smoking desert and salt pillar, are a memorial of their folly. "Pentapolis" refers to the five cities of the plain (Gen 14:1-12).

so that they could not even be
hidden in their fall.
⁹But Wisdom rescued from tribula-
tions those who served her.

¹⁰She, when a righteous man fled
from his brother's anger,
guided him in right ways,
Showed him the kingdom of God
and gave him knowledge of
holy things;
She prospered him in his labors
and made abundant the fruit of
his works,
¹¹Stood by him against the greed of
his defrauders,
and enriched him;
¹²She preserved him from foes,
and secured him against ambush,
And she gave him the prize for his
hard struggle
that he might know that devotion to God is mightier
than all else.

¹³She did not abandon a righteous
man when he was sold,
but rescued him from sin.
¹⁴She went down with him into the
dungeon,
and did not desert him in his
bonds,
Until she brought him the scepter of
royalty
and authority over his oppressors,
Proved false those who had defamed
him,
and gave him eternal glory.

¹⁵The holy people and their blameless descendants—it was she
who rescued them from the nation
that oppressed them.
¹⁶She entered the soul of the Lord's
servant,
and withstood fearsome kings
with signs and wonders;
¹⁷she gave the holy ones the reward of their labors,

10:10-12 Jacob

The story of Jacob is concise but complete. "[K]ingdom of God," the only Old Testament instance of the phrase familiar from the New Testament, refers to Jacob's dream of the stairway to the heavens, with angels going up and down on it, and the Lord standing beside him and promising him land and descendants (Gen 28:12-15). Jacob's devotion gave him the prize in his struggle with the night visitor (Gen 32:23-33).

10:13-14 Joseph

The story ends when Joseph attains power in Egypt. The midrashic style is highly selective. Nothing is said, for example, about the bitter relationship of the brothers to Joseph or its resolution. Joseph's "scepter of royalty" prefigures the authority the entire people will later have over Egypt.

10:15-21 Moses

The emphasis changes from person to people, for verse 15 is concerned with "the holy people and that blameless race." Moses appears briefly in verse 16, and thereafter the people are the subject or objects of all subsequent

45

Conducted them by a wondrous road,
became a shelter for them by day a starry flame by night.
[18]She took them across the Red Sea and brought them through the deep waters.
[19]Their enemies she overwhelmed, and churned them up from the bottom of the depths.

---

verbs. The Red Sea is mentioned explicitly, another place the text makes a specific reference instead of relying on type. The emphasis falls on the same elements of the exodus as will later be singled out in chapters 11 and 15–19, the journey through the sea and through the wilderness. The allusion to the singing of God's praises is to Exodus 15, the Song of the Sea.

THE EXODUS: GOD PROVIDES FOR HIS CHILD ISRAEL

11:1–19:22

Part 1 described in schematic fashion how wisdom, the hidden energy of the world, protects the child of God, and how it becomes visible, especially when the child is threatened by the wicked. Part 2 showed what wisdom is, how to attain it, and its embodiment in a succession of righteous historical personages. Part 3 shifts the perspective by speaking of God rather than of wisdom. God is named as the one who guides and protects the righteous child, Israel. Wisdom is mentioned only twice in part 3, both times in connection with the origin of idolatry (14:2, 5). The shift from wisdom to God is less radical than it might seem, however, for wisdom represents the outreach of God to human beings. Another shift is that the child of God, who was left unidentified in part 1 (2:13, 16; 5:1), is now identified with Israel (18:13; 19:6).

Part 3 also contains two digressions on questions relevant to the theme of God's governance: (1) how could a "philanthropic" (= "people-loving") God destroy the Canaanite inhabitants of Palestine and give their land to Israel? and (2) how ought one evaluate other religions?

Part 3 is the most specifically Israelite part of the book. Up to this point, the author has dealt with "the nations," i.e., the human race generally. Part 1 is about the typical righteous and wicked person, and is addressed to "kings" (= Gentile kings and their subjects). Part 2 is about wisdom and how anyone can attain it, though an Israelite is the model king. Ancient Near Eastern wisdom literature had in view humankind as such; national consciousness did not generally play a large role. In Proverbs, Job, and Ecclesiastes, Israelite heroes and institutions are not mentioned. Only with

²⁰Therefore the righteous despoiled
the wicked;
and they sang of your holy name,
Lord,

and praised in unison your con-
quering hand,
²¹Because Wisdom opened the mouths
of the mute,
and gave ready speech to infants.

Sirach (first quarter of the second century B.C.) do specifically Israelite themes appear. Like Sirach, Wisdom of Solomon similarly combines universal and national themes.

The author portrays Israel in its defining moment, the exodus. In ancient Near Eastern cultures, the moment of origin was deemed particularly important, for it was then that the imprint of the creating gods was clearest. In antiquity, people thought of the world as "given" at the beginning, having already the institutions (kingship, temples, marriage, etc.) and systems of the present. To understand a reality, therefore, one had to understand its founding moment. Hence, the founding moment of Israel, the exodus, took on a special importance.

The Israelite exodus is explained in a seemingly strange way—as seven plagues. In the book of Exodus, the exodus is a two-part process involving liberation and formation—the people cease serving Pharaoh in Egypt and begin serving Yahweh in Canaan. The ten plagues in Exodus 7–11 are viewed as a series of battles between Yahweh and Pharaoh in which the tenth, the death of the Egyptian firstborn, is the climax that signals victory for Yahweh. Why did Wisdom of Solomon take a relatively minor part of the story and make it *the* story? One reason is that the book can presume its readers are sufficiently familiar with the story so it can concentrate on one aspect. The major reason, however, seems to be that the plagues show the working of divine justice (rewarding the just and punishing the wicked) as divine control of nature. The judgment scene in 5:16-23 told how God "shall arm creation to requite the enemy" (5:17) and "the universe will war with him against the ungodly" (5:20). The plagues (to which Wisdom adds some wilderness miracles) illustrate God using creation to protect his child (Israel) against the wicked (Egypt).

Wisdom 11:6-14 and chapters 16–19 compare the effects of the seven plagues on Israel and Egypt. In addition, there is another system alongside the seven comparisons—five sketches showing how Egypt's faulty reasoning led them into an act that turned out to have bad consequences for them. Each sketch is introduced by the Greek preposition *anti*, "instead of, in return for" (11:6, 15; 16:2, 20; 18:3). At times, a sketch blends with a comparison.

11 ¹She prospered their affairs
    through the holy prophet.

III: Special Providence of
God During the Exodus

Introduction

²They journeyed through the unin-
    habited desert,
and in lonely places they pitched
    their tents;
³they withstood enemies and
    warded off their foes.
⁴When they thirsted, they called
    upon you,

and water was given them from
    the sheer rock,
a quenching of their thirst from
    the hard stone.
⁵For by the things through which
    their foes were punished
they in their need were benefited.

First Example:
Water Punishes the Egyptians and
Benefits the Israelites

⁶Instead of a river's perennial source,
    troubled with impure blood
⁷as a rebuke to the decree for the
    slaying of infants,

11:1-5 Protection in the wilderness; the principle of divine activity

The first verse makes the transition from Moses the wisdom hero to Moses the leader of the exodus, which will be the topic henceforth. Before dealing with the exodus plagues, the author mentions the journey through the wilderness, which took place *after* the plagues. In the Bible, the wilderness is the environment most inhospitable to human beings. Miracles are required for humans to live there—bread from heaven (Exod 16:4; Neh 9:15), water from the rock (Num 20:8; Deut 8:15), valleys raised and mountains lowered (Isa 40:4). Great acts of God were required for Israel to survive (Wis 11:2-4). In that extraordinary period, the divine acts that benefited Israel were the same acts that punished their enemies (11:5). Verse 5 is important because it states succinctly the principle that will operate in the seven comparisons: by the act that benefits Israel, God punishes their foes. Actually, the principle has been operative so far in the book up to this point, e.g., in chapters 2 and 5, the death of the just person was at once his entry into eternal life and his killer's condemnation.

Comparisons of Egyptians and Israelites during the Exodus (11:6-14)

11:6-14 Comparison one: flowing water

The first of the seven comparisons (Greek *synkrasis*) between Egypt and Israel is the Nile turned into blood (the first plague, Exod 7:14-25) and the water given to Israel in the wilderness (Exod 17:1-7; Num 20:2-13). In the structure of the book, two digressions (11:15–12:27; chapters 13–15) will

"When they thirsted, they called upon Moses, and water was given them from the sheer rock" (Wisdom 11:4).

You gave them abundant water
beyond their hope,
⁸after you had shown by the thirst
they experienced
how you punished their adver-
saries.
⁹For when they had been tried, though
only mildly chastised,
they recognized how the wicked,
condemned in anger,
were being tormented.
¹⁰You tested your own people, ad-
monishing them as a father;
but as a stern king you probed and
condemned the wicked.
¹¹Those near and far were equally
afflicted:

¹²for a twofold grief took hold of
them
and a groaning at the remem-
brance of the ones who
had departed.
¹³For when they heard that the cause
of their own torments
was a benefit to these others, they
recognized the Lord.
¹⁴For though they had mocked and
rejected him who had been
cast out and abandoned long
ago,
in the final outcome, they mar-
veled at him,
since their thirst proved unlike
that of the righteous.

---

subsequently intervene before the second comparison in 16:1-4. Each of the seven comparisons illustrates the principle of divine justice enunciated in 11:5 and operative throughout the book.

The main difference is that the Nile ("the perennial river," 11:6), the sole source of water in Egypt, became undrinkable whereas there was abundant water in the desert. The Nile becoming bloody was punishment for Pharaoh's decree that every Hebrew boy was to be thrown into the Nile (Exod 1:22). The figure of Moses opens and closes the section. Moses is implicitly in Wisdom 11:7a, for he was one of the boys thrown into the Nile (Exod 2:1-4), and explicitly in Wisdom 11:14, for he is the one cast out and abandoned long ago. The author addresses a problem for anyone making the case that God is just, i.e., punishes the wicked and rewards the good. The problem is that the good often suffer; in this case Israel suffered from thirst in the wilderness. The author's answer (11:9) is that such suffering is only temporary and it has an educational purpose: to teach the people how the wicked were being chastised, i.e., the Egyptians were suffering a deadly drought.

In verse 7, the author begins to address God in the second person singular; previously God was addressed as "you" only in the great prayer in chapter 9. From now on, however, God will frequently be addressed as "you" as the narrator turns the events of the exodus into praise. In 11:10a, God is a "father" to the Israelites and a "stern king" to the Egyptians. Both metaphors relate to the purpose of suffering. "Father," derived from Prov-

Second Example:
Animals Punish the Egyptians and
Benefit the Israelites

¹⁵In return for their senseless, wicked
thoughts,
which misled them into worshiping dumb serpents and
worthless insects,
You sent upon them swarms of dumb
creatures for vengeance;

¹⁶that they might recognize that
one is punished by the
very things through
which one sins.

Digression on God's Mercy

¹⁷For not without means was your
almighty hand,
that had fashioned the universe
from formless matter,

erbs 3:12 ("For whom the Lord loves he reproves, and he chastises [like a father] the son he favors"), shows that Israel's sufferings are educational, teaching them about God's rule. "Stern king" shows that Egypt's sufferings are punishment for their wickedness.

The author's interest in psychology is particularly clear in 11:12-14, which explains the emotional discontent that increased the Egyptians' pain—the drinking water they were deprived of by the bloodying of the Nile was freely available to their enemies in the wilderness, the leader they had tried to remove turned out to be successful. The recognition leads to "shame" in that one loses face because what one hoped in has turned out to be false.

The First Digression:
The Moderation and Mercy of God (11:15–12:27)

The mention of the animals worshiped by the Egyptians in 11:15 pro-vokes the thought that God could, in poetic justice, have employed the most vicious animals ("bears," "fierce lions," 11:17) instantaneously to tear the worshipers apart. Instead, God acted mercifully, allowing time for the repentance that wins mercy and forgiveness (11:21–12:2). The digression then turns to another traditional enemy of Israel, the Canaanites (12:3-11). "The ancient inhabitants of your holy land," though sinners to their core (12:3-11), were not wiped out at one blow, but were "sent wasps as forerun-ners of your army" (Wis 12:8; cf. Exod 23:28; Deut 7:20; Josh 24:12) to warn them so they would repent. There follows a reflection on divine sovereignty and mercy in Wisdom 12:12-18. The section up to this point is developed with perfect symmetry: the Egyptians (11:15-20) and God's response of mercy rather than immediate punishment (11:21–12:2); the Canaanites (12:3-11) and God's response of mercy rather than immediate punishment

to send upon them many bears
   or fierce lions,
[18]Or newly created, wrathful, unknown beasts
   breathing forth fiery breath,
Or pouring out roaring smoke,
   or flashing terrible sparks from
   their eyes.
[19]Not only could these attack and
   completely destroy them;
   even their frightful appearance
   itself could slay.
[20]Even without these, they could have
   been killed at a single blast,
   pursued by justice
   and winnowed by your mighty
   spirit.
But you have disposed all things by
   measure and number and
   weight.
[21]For great strength is always present
   with you;
   who can resist the might of your
   arm?

[22]Indeed, before you the whole
   universe is like a grain from
   a balance,
   or a drop of morning dew come
   down upon the earth.

[23]But you have mercy on all, because
   you can do all things;
   and you overlook sins for the
   sake of repentance.
[24]For you love all things that are
   and loathe nothing that you have
   made;
   for you would not fashion what
   you hate.
[25]How could a thing remain, unless
   you willed it;
   or be preserved, had it not been
   called forth by you?
[26]But you spare all things, because
   they are yours,
   O Ruler and Lover of souls,

12 [1]for your imperishable spirit is
   in all things!

(12:12-18). The conclusion of the section is the double lesson Israel should take from these events (12:19-27).

11:15–12:2 Opportunity for repentance of Egypt

The opening preposition, "in return for" (Greek: *anti*), introduces another instance of poetic justice (one is punished by the very thing through which one sins, 11:16). In this sketch, the Egyptians' animal worship (11:15) provokes God to send animals to punish them. The punishment has a point, however—"that they might recognize [God's hand]" (11:16a). God could have sent the most vicious animals, bears or lions, to kill at one stroke (11:17-20), but sent instead the smaller animals of the plagues, frogs (16:1-4; see Exod 8:1-15) and the flies and locusts (16:5-14; see Exod 8:16-32) that hurt but do not kill, allowing the Egyptians time for repentance. One reason for moderation is God's careful, almost mathematically exact, governance (11:20-22). The same notion occurs in other Jewish literature (1 Enoch 72-82; 2 Esdr 4:36-37) and in Hellenistic writings such as Plato's *Laws* 575B and

²Therefore you rebuke offenders
little by little,
warn them, and remind them of
the sins they are commit-
ting,
that they may abandon their
wickedness and believe
in you, Lord!
³For truly, the ancient inhabitants of
your holy land,
⁴whom you hated for deeds most
odious—
works of sorcery and impious
sacrifices;
⁵These merciless murderers of
children,
devourers of human flesh,
and initiates engaged in a blood
ritual,
⁶and parents who took with their
own hands defenseless
lives,

You willed to destroy by the hands
of our ancestors,
⁷that the land that is dearest of
all to you
might receive a worthy colony
of God's servants.
⁸But even these you spared, since
they were but mortals
and sent wasps as forerunners of
your army
that they might exterminate them
by degrees.

⁹Not that you were without power to
have the wicked vanquished
in battle by the righteous,
or wiped out at once by terrible
beasts or by one decisive
word;
¹⁰But condemning them by degrees,
you gave them space for
repentance.

Philo's *On Dreams* 2.193. The second reason is more specifically biblical, and especially dear to the author of Wisdom (1:13-15; 2:22-24)—God's loving commitment to creation, and willingness to give human beings the opportunity to repent and be renewed (11:23–12:2). Not all religious thinkers of the time were so positive regarding God's abiding commitment and the possibility of human renewal. Some Qumran sectarians, for example, viewed outsiders with harshness and suspicion and emphasized divine vengeance.

12:3-18 Opportunity for repentance of Canaan

The author is unusually negative in assessing the conduct of the Canaanites. The reason perhaps is that the Israelite conquest was used in anti-Jewish polemic of the time as a sign of Jewish injustice and cruelty. The author, understandably, stresses the Canaanite practice of infant sacrifice, attested in Phoenicia, pre-exilic Israel, and the Phoenician colonies in North Africa. Polluted by such conduct, Canaan would be ennobled by "a worthy colony of God's children" (Greek = "children/servants of God" 12:7). Countering pagan criticism, the author emphasizes Israel's God is

You were not unaware that their
origins were wicked
and their malice ingrained,
And that their dispositions would
never change;
¹¹for they were a people accursed
from the beginning.
Neither out of fear for anyone
did you grant release from their
sins.
¹²For who can say to you, "What have
you done?"
or who can oppose your decree?
Or when peoples perish, who can
challenge you, their maker;
or who can come into your
presence to vindicate the
unrighteous?
¹³For neither is there any god besides
you who have the care of all,
that you need show you have
not unjustly condemned;
¹⁴Nor can any king or prince con-
front you on behalf of those
you have punished.

¹⁵But as you are righteous, you
govern all things righteously;
you regard it as unworthy of your
power
to punish one who has incurred
no blame.
¹⁶For your might is the source of
righteousness;
your mastery over all things makes
you lenient to all.
¹⁷For you show your might when
the perfection of your power
is disbelieved;
and in those who know you, you
rebuke insolence.
¹⁸But though you are master of might,
you judge with clemency,
and with much lenience you
govern us;
for power, whenever you will,
attends you.

¹⁹You taught your people, by these
deeds,
that those who are righteous must
be kind;

---

absolute and above human criticism (12:12-18). Yet the Canaanites, wicked as they were, had the opportunity to repent (12:8-11). It is always interesting to see how a later biblical author interprets an early reference. "Wasps," mentioned in Exodus 23:28 as a messenger of destruction preceding the Israelite armies, is reinterpreted in Wisdom 11:15-16 as a small animal punishing the Canaanites for their animal worship.

12:19-27 The double lesson for Israel

"Your people" (12:19) is contrasted with the people of Egypt and Ca-naan. "These deeds" are the divine acts that first warned and only afterward inflicted punishment, and giving an opportunity for repentance. The reason for the two-step process is given in verse 19b, literally, "because the just one must be philanthropic [= loving humanity]." God is preeminently just (12:15) and God's actions are "philanthropic" in providing an opportunity for repentance (Greek *metanoia*, 12:19c). God is a teacher, however, whose

And you gave your children reason
to hope
that you would allow them to
repent for their sins.
²⁰For these were enemies of your
servants, doomed to death;
yet, while you punished them
with such solicitude and
indulgence,
granting time and opportunity
to abandon wickedness,
²¹With what exactitude you judged
your children,
to whose ancestors you gave the
sworn covenants of
goodly promises!
²²Therefore to give us a lesson you
punish our enemies with
measured deliberation
so that we may think earnestly
of your goodness when
we judge,
and, when being judged, we may
look for mercy.

Second Example Resumed

²³Hence those unrighteous who lived
a life of folly,
you tormented through their own
abominations.
²⁴For they went far astray in the paths
of error,
taking for gods the worthless
and disgusting among
beasts,
being deceived like senseless
infants.
²⁵Therefore as though upon unreason-
ing children,
you sent your judgment on them
as a mockery;
²⁶But they who took no heed of a
punishment which was but
child's play
were to experience a condemnation worthy of God.
²⁷For by the things through which
they suffered distress,

actions instruct Israel while punishing their enemies (12:21). Israel learns about God by watching God act in history. Like other wisdom books, Wisdom of Solomon puts a premium on learning through the "discipline" of the teacher.

Wisdom 12:23-27 returns to the principles stated at the beginning of the digression (11:15-16)—people are punished through the choices they make (cf. 12:23, 27), and worship of animals brings punishment by means of animals (see 12:24). In keeping with the Platonic philosophical tradition, the author sees virtue as right thinking and vice as faulty knowing. The unjust are foolish (12:24), they go astray on the paths of error and are deceived (12:24). Only at the end do they see and recognize "the true God whom formerly they had refused to know" (v. 27). Inability to see and know the nature of reality is also the fault of the wicked in chapter 2; only when they see the exaltation of the just person whom they persecuted (Wis 5) do they recognize the true God whose actions they had failed to perceive.

being tortured by the very things
they deemed gods,
They saw and recognized the true
God whom formerly they
had refused to know;
with this, their final condemnation came upon them.

Digression on False Worship

A. Nature Worship

13 ¹Foolish by nature were all who
were in ignorance of God,
and who from the good things
seen did not succeed in
knowing the one who is,

and from studying the works did
not discern the artisan;
²Instead either fire, or wind, or the
swift air,
or the circuit of the stars, or the
mighty water,
or the luminaries of heaven, the
governors of the world,
they considered gods.
³Now if out of joy in their beauty
they thought them gods,
let them know how far more
excellent is the Lord than
these;
for the original source of beauty
fashioned them.

The Second Digression: False Worship (Wisdom 13–15)

Since the goal of Wisdom of Solomon is to persuade people, especially the Jewish community, of the nobility and truth of Judaism, the author has to point out the defects of other religions. In that market place of ideas, proponents of one religion had to make a case for its superiority over others. The author concentrates on a single theme—the object of worship, evidently presuming that the god one worships is the key to any religion. The author's division of the forms of cultic worship was common in Hellenistic commentary of the time. Philo makes a similar distinction between the worship of natural elements and of idols or animals in *On the Decalogue* 52 and *On the Special Laws* 1:13.

There are three critiques: (1) unreflective nature worship (13:1-9); (2) the worship of images (13:1–15:13); (3) the worship of images and animals (15:14-19). The first and the last are of approximately the same length, whereas the middle section is long and complex. The criticism becomes increasingly severe as the objects of worship become more reprehensible. Those in the first group are "foolish" (13:1), those in the second are "wretched" (13:10), and those in the third are "most stupid of all and worse than senseless" (15:14).

13:1-9 The critique of the philosophers

The critique is concerned with right and wrong knowing, as one might expect in a book in the Platonic tradition. The philosophers' basic fault is

⁴Or if they were struck by their might
and energy,
let them realize from these things
how much more powerful
is the one who made them.
⁵For from the greatness and the
beauty of created things
their original author, by analogy,
is seen.
⁶But yet, for these the blame is less;
For they have gone astray perhaps,
though they seek God and wish
to find him.

⁷For they search busily among his
works,
but are distracted by what they
see, because the things
seen are fair.
⁸But again, not even these are
pardonable.
⁹For if they so far succeeded in
knowledge
that they could speculate about
the world,
how did they not more quickly
find its Lord?

that "studying the works [they] did not discern the artisan" (13:1). Though their incorrect knowledge is here judged leniently, it is essentially the same fault as the violent gang in chapter 2 who did not know the just person was the child of God. The great difference between chapters 2 and 13 is that the unknowing philosophers "seek God and wish to find him" (13:6), whereas the unknowing gang does not, and plots to kill the child of God (2:12-20). The faulty knowledge of the philosophers is underscored: they are "in ignorance of God," "did not succeed in knowing," "did not discern" (v. 1), "considered" the elements gods (v. 2), etc. They did not know rightly, however, for they never went beyond sense impressions to reflect that the creator is seen in his works (vv. 1, 3-5). Verse 7 is the core. Having conceded in verse 6 that the philosophers sincerely seek God, the author is precise about their failure, literally translated as, "for, engaged with his works, they search / and are misled by the seeing because what they see is beautiful." To paraphrase, they are misled by over-reliance on sense impressions and by failure to reflect. Wisdom of Solomon repeatedly states an unseen world coexists with the world of daily experience. The philosophers stop at the world of daily experience, seduced by its beauty.

Does the author refer to a specific group who are "in ignorance of God"? The philosopher Philo's similar critique (*On the Decalogue* 52–54) clearly refers to Stoicism. They regarded the world as an enclosed system, and explained it without recourse to Platonic other-worldliness. Stoics were pantheists; god, who guides the world toward good, is present in everything as "spirit," conceived however in corporeal terms, for only the corporeal exists. The Stoics took nature as their guide, and it is easy to see why

B. Idolatry	The Carpenter and Wooden Idols
[10]But wretched are they, and in dead things are their hopes, who termed gods things made by human hands: Gold and silver, the product of art, and images of beasts, or useless stone, the work of an ancient hand.	[11]A carpenter may cut down a suitable tree and skillfully scrape off all its bark, And deftly plying his art produce something fit for daily use,

"natural law" originated with them. Wisdom of Solomon faults them for the philosophical materialism that makes them reject the hidden world advocated by the book. It also faults them for failing to see the universe as *created* by a being outside and greater than it, "the one who is," "the artisan" (13:1). "The one who is" is the same phrase found in Exodus 3:14, "I AM who am."

The kind of critique in this passage is used by Paul in Romans 1:18-23 to indict the Gentiles for failing to worship God: "Ever since the creation of the world, his invisible attributes of eternal power and divinity have been able to be understood and perceived in what he has made. As a result they have no excuse" (Rom 1:20). The body of knowledge that may be obtained by human reason alone is sometimes contrasted with "revealed theology." The distinction was worked out in the Middle Ages and is reflected in a definition of Vatican I in 1869. Reformation theology tends to reject the possibility of natural theology because of what it regards as the incapacity of fallen human nature to grasp such truths.

13:10–15:13 Worshipers of images

Unlike the short and simple first and third sections of the digression, the middle section is long and complex, shaped by a chiastic structure (a pattern where the second half of the argument is a parallel but inverted form of the one that comes before): A. 13:10-19, wooden images; B. 14:1-10, invocation of God, reference to history; C. 14:11-31, chastisement; B'. 15:1-6, invocation of God, reference to history; A'. 15:7-13, clay images.

13:10-19 Wooden images and their makers

The Greek word for this kind of false worshiper literally means "suffering hardship; toiling; wretched." "Wretched" is more severe than "foolish" (13:1), but less severe than the final judgment, "most stupid of all and worse than senseless in mind" (15:14). The first commandment of the Decalogue

"The worker beseeches for travel something that cannot even walk" (Wisdom 13:18).

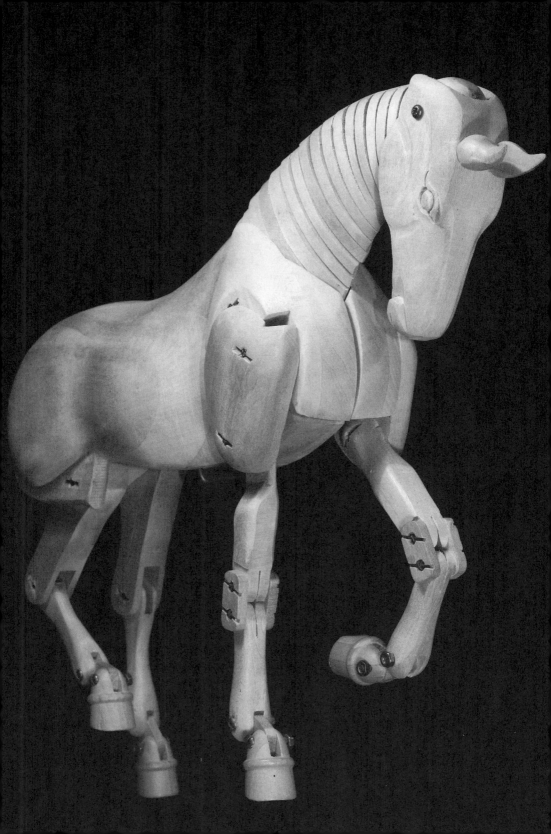

¹²And use the scraps from his handi-
work
in preparing his food, and have
his fill;
¹³Then the good-for-nothing refuse
from these remnants,
crooked wood grown full of knots,
he takes and carves to occupy his
spare time.
This wood he models with mindless
skill,
and patterns it on the image of a
human being
¹⁴or makes it resemble some
worthless beast.
When he has daubed it with red and
crimsoned its surface with
red stain,
and daubed over every blemish
in it,
¹⁵He makes a fitting shrine for it

and puts it on the wall, fastening
it with a nail.
¹⁶Thus he provides for it lest it fall
down,
knowing that it cannot help itself;
for, truly, it is an image and needs
help.
¹⁷But when he prays about his goods
or marriage or children,
he is not ashamed to address the
thing without a soul.
For vigor he invokes the powerless;
¹⁸for life he entreats the dead;
For aid he beseeches the wholly
incompetent;
for travel, something that cannot
even walk;
¹⁹For profit in business and success
with his hands
he asks power of a thing with
hands utterly powerless.

---

forbids images: "You shall not have other gods beside me. You shall not make for yourself an idol or a likeness of anything in the heavens above or on the earth below or in the waters beneath the earth; you shall not bow down before them or serve them" (Exod 20:3-5; Deut 5:7-9). The absolute prohibition inspired a vehement polemic against images, e.g., Psalm 115:4-8; Jeremiah 10:1-16; Isaiah 40:18-20; 41:6-7; 44:9-20. This passage draws on that tradition, especially Isaiah 44:9-20.

More blameworthy than the philosophers who worshiped natural phenomena (13:1-9), image-worshipers adore what their hands have made, fashioning inanimate material, gold, silver, stone (13:10), and wood. The last-mentioned, wood, is the author's chief concern in verses 11-19. It is the least permanent material, scrap wood useless for anything else. It is unsuitable as an image of god, for the wood must be laboriously carved simply to make it resemble a human being. When it has attained a human shape, it is utterly passive. Though immovable, people pray to the statue for help; though inanimate, people turn to it for vitality. In brief, image worship is irrational and utterly contrary to the true wisdom espoused by the book.

14 ¹Again, one preparing for a
voyage and about to traverse
the wild waves
cries out to wood more unsound
than the boat that bears
him.
²For the urge for profits devised this
latter,
and Wisdom the artisan produced
it.

³But your providence, O Father!
guides it,
for you have furnished even in
the sea a road,
and through the waves a steady
path,

⁴Showing that you can save from any
danger,
so that even one without skill
may embark.
⁵But you will that the products of
your Wisdom be not idle;
therefore people trust their lives
even to most frail wood,
and were safe crossing the waves
on a raft.
⁶For of old, when the proud giants
were being destroyed,
the hope of the universe, who
took refuge on a raft,
left to the world a future for the
human family, under the
guidance of your hand.

14:1-10 God, not images, is friend and benefactor to human beings

The topic of the previous section is continued. According to the author, to embark on a sea voyage is a daring act, for one entrusts oneself to a small wooden boat floating on the wild and unpredictable deep. To allay their fears and obtain protection for the voyage, people pray to a wooden image. The text may refer to images of Castor and Pollux, twin heroes in classical mythology, the Dioscuri. Castor was the son of Leda and Tyndareus, and Pollux was the son of Leda and Zeus; the half-brothers were famous for their exploits and devotion to each other. Saint Cyril of Alexandria (d. 444) says that Alexandrians put pictures of the twins to the right and left of prows of ships. How, asks the author (14:1), can one entrust oneself to a wooden image more fragile than the ship that carries it? What actually guides a ship over the threatening sea is not a paltry wooden image, but "your providence, O Father!" (14:3).

The author selects a particularly hazardous enterprise, commercial sailing in the Mediterranean, to show the foolishness of human behavior. Instead of recognizing the one power that can protect and guide them, sailors rather pin their hopes on wooden images that are far more frail than any boat. The author in no way denigrates the trades of shipbuilding or sailing, for wisdom inspires people to practice them (14:2, 5). The world is good (1:14) and intended to be developed. God gives wisdom to humans precisely

⁷For blest is the wood through which
    righteousness comes about;
⁸but the handmade idol is
    accursed, and its maker
    as well:
he for having produced it, and
    the corruptible thing,
    because it was termed a
    god.
⁹Equally odious to God are the evil-
    doer and the evil deed;
¹⁰and the thing made will be
    punished with its maker.
¹¹Therefore upon even the idols of
    the nations shall a judgment
    come,

since they became abominable
    among God's works,
Snares for human souls
    and a trap for the feet of the
    senseless.

The Origin and Evils of Idolatry

¹²For the source of wantonness is the ▶
    devising of idols;
and their invention, a corruption
    of life.
¹³For in the beginning they were not,
    nor can they ever continue;
¹⁴for from human emptiness they
    came into the world,

---

that they might act wisely even in the most challenging and difficult enter-
prises. An example of someone successfully entrusting himself to a piece
of wood is Noah (14:5-7; see Gen 6–9) who made an ark to escape the flood
sent to wipe out the inhabitants of the world. But the wooden image and
its maker will not be saved (14:8-10).

Two stylistic points are noteworthy, the address to God in the second
person and the designation "Father" for God. The section, like its parallel
section in the chiasm (15:1-6), refers to God as "you" (14:3, 5). The section
is otherwise in third-person narrative style; the abrupt shift lends intimacy
to the passages. Addressing God directly as "Father" develops the metaphor of God as the father who educates his son or disciple by discipline
(Prov 3:12). By addressing God as father here, the author assumes the
mantle of the just person mentioned in chapter 2 and of Israel that will be
explicitly identified as God's child in Wisdom 18:13.

Though 14:7, "blest is the wood through which justice comes about,"
actually refers to the ark of Noah, some patristic authors took it as a reference to the wood of the cross by which the world was saved. The Greek
word used here, *xulon*, is used for the cross in New Testament passages
such as Acts 5:30 and Galatians 3:13.

14:11-31 The origin and effects of image worship

The beginning (14:11-12) and the end (14:30-31) of the passage predict
divine judgment on idolaters, for the Scriptures condemn false worship.

and therefore a sudden end is
devised for them.

¹⁵For a father, afflicted with untimely
mourning,
made an image of the child so
quickly taken from him,
And now honored as a god what
once was dead
and handed down to his house-
hold mysteries and sacri-
fices.
¹⁶Then, in the course of time, the
impious practice gained
strength and was observed
as law,
and graven things were worshiped
by royal decrees.
¹⁷People who lived so far away that
they could not honor him in
his presence
copied the appearance of the
distant king
And made a public image of him
they wished to honor,
out of zeal to flatter the absent
one as though present.

¹⁸And to promote this observance
among those to whom it was
strange,
the artisan's ambition provided
a stimulus.
¹⁹For he, perhaps in his determina-
tion to please the ruler,
labored over the likeness to the
best of his skill;
²⁰And the masses, drawn by the
charm of the workmanship,
soon took as an object of worship
the one who shortly
before was honored as a
human being.
²¹And this became a snare for the
world,
that people enslaved to either
grief or tyranny
conferred the incommunicable
Name on stones and
wood.

²²Then it was not enough for them to
err in their knowledge of God;
but even though they live in a
great war resulting from
ignorance,

Between the two sets of verses, the author describes the origin of image worship and the malice it provokes in those who practice it.

To show that images are wrong and pervert created objects to unnatural uses, the author gives a historical sketch of the rise of image worship. Image worship did not exist from the beginning, i.e., it is not "natural." Its origin can be assigned to two sources. It should be noted that in antiquity, writers often sought ultimate explanations in accounts of how a reality appeared for the first time, for the first appearance of something provided a privileged glimpse of its purpose. One origin of image worship was an incident in which a beloved son died prematurely, and the grieving father made an image by which to remember him The image eventually became worshiped as a god (14:15-16). Another source of image-worship was also a specific

they call such evils peace.
²³For while they practice either child
sacrifices or occult mysteries,
or frenzied carousing in exotic
rites,
²⁴They no longer respect either lives
or purity of marriage;
but they either waylay and kill
each other, or aggrieve
each other by adultery.
²⁵And all is confusion—blood and
murder, theft and guile,
corruption, faithlessness, turmoil,
perjury,
²⁶Disturbance of good people, neglect
of gratitude,
besmirching of souls, unnatural
lust,
disorder in marriage, adultery
and shamelessness.

²⁷For the worship of infamous idols
is the reason and source and
extreme of all evil.

²⁸For they either go mad with enjoy-
ment, or prophesy lies,
or live lawlessly or lightly perjure
themselves.
²⁹For as their trust is in lifeless idols,
they expect no harm when they
have sworn falsely.
³⁰But on both counts justice shall
overtake them:
because they thought perversely
of God by devoting them-
selves to idols,
and because they deliberately
swore false oaths, despis-
ing piety.
³¹For it is not the might of those by
whom they swear,

situation: in a country far from the dwelling of the king, his loyal subjects decided to honor his portrait in lieu of his person. Eager artisans encouraged the trade in images and, lo and behold, the king became a god (14:17-20). The origin of the worship of images is therefore shameful, arising from grief or greed (14:21, see also 14:13-14).

Wisdom 14:22 begins to describe the great evils that come upon idolaters, even though they themselves may not be aware they are suffering. Verse 22 expresses a sentiment remarkably close to a famous comment of the Roman historian Tacitus (56–ca. a.d. 120) on the Roman Empire: "To plunder, butcher, steal, these things they misname empire; they make a desolation and they call it peace" (*Agricola* 30). The following verses show the effects of such an unrecognized "war" upon the "combatants": they fall into corrupt practices such as child-sacrifice and orgies (14:23), adultery and murder (14:34), and a riot of passions and crimes in verses 25-26. The list of vices show that the worship of images is the cause of every evil (14:27). Retribution will come not from the lifeless images, but from the living God who is offended by the people swearing by them (14:29-31).

but the just retribution of sinners,
that ever follows upon the transgression of the wicked.

15 ¹But you, our God, are good and
true,
slow to anger, and governing all
with mercy.
²For even if we sin, we are yours, and
know your might;
but we will not sin, knowing that
we belong to you.

³For to know you well is complete
righteousness,
and to know your might is the
root of immortality.
⁴For the evil creation of human fancy
did not deceive us,
nor the fruitless labor of painters,
A form smeared with varied colors,
⁵the sight of which arouses yearn-
ing in a fool,
till he longs for the inanimate
form of a dead image.

15:1-6 God, not images, is friend and benefactor to human beings

The section balances 14:1-10, which is also concerned with showing that it is God and not images who benefits the human race. After the grim description of image-worshipers and their depravities, the affectionate second-person address to the living God in 15:1-2 comes as a relief, "But you, our God, are good and true" and "we are yours." The author identifies himself with the people of God, "you, *our* God" (emphasis added). The passage is after all about the one God who is also the God of Israel, and the speaker is a member of this people. As was true in the previous section, the worshiper is transformed by the object of worship, "to know you well is complete justice" (15:3). Worshipers are no longer deceived by the forms and colors that stir up false hopes (15:4-5), which was the case with those venerating images. In sum, 15:1-6 is a warm and enthusiastic restatement of the biblical injunction to worship God alone, without using images. They are also thoroughly compatible with the Platonic philosophic tradition that distinguished earthly form and heavenly reality.

The four divine attributes that the section singles out in verse 1, "good and true, slow to anger, and governing all with mercy," are inspired by a famous passage in Exodus 34:6-7, "So the Lord passed before him and proclaimed, 'The LORD, the LORD, a God gracious and merciful, slow to anger and abounding in love and fidelity, continuing his love for a thousand generations . . .'" The context of the exodus confession was people's apostasy—worshiping the golden calf (an image) and God's decision to destroy them for the violation. When Moses intercedes, God relents and acts with mercy. The scene has influenced the Wisdom passage. Wisdom 14:11-31 described worship of images and the depravity that results (cf. Exod 32:6).

⁶Lovers of evil things, and worthy of
  such hopes
are they who make them and
    long for them and
    worship them.

The Potter's Clay Idols

⁷For the potter, laboriously working
  the soft earth,
molds for our service each single
    article:
He fashions out of the same clay
    both the vessels that serve for
    clean purposes
  and their opposites, all alike;
As to what shall be the use of each
    vessel of either class
  the worker in clay is the judge.

⁸With misspent toil he molds a
    meaningless god from the
    selfsame clay,
  though he himself shortly
    before was made from
    the earth,
And is soon to go whence he was
  taken,
  when the life that was lent him
    is demanded back.
⁹But his concern is not that he is to
  die
  nor that his span of life is brief;
Rather, he vies with goldsmiths and
    silversmiths
  and emulates molders of bronze,
  and takes pride in fashioning
    counterfeits.

Yet the Lord is merciful and loyal, restoring the broken relationship in Exodus 34:6, and here as well.

15:7-13 Clay images and their makers

In the chiastic structure of 13:10–15:13, the denunciation of makers of clay images matches that of makers of wooden images in 13:10-19. Though both sections mention makers of gold and silver images (13:10cd and 15:9cd), their chief concern is wood and clay images, and these materials provide the occasion for the rich ironies of the passages. The potter is implicitly contrasted with the Divine Potter who molds human beings and gives them life (e.g., Gen 2:7; Isa 43:1; 45:7, 9; 49:5; Jer 18:1-11; Sir 33:13). The human potter in contrast makes only lifeless objects. The potter "creates" from the very clay he or she was taken from only a short time before, and will return there soon (15:8). Bedazzled by greed, the potter competes with those who work in gold and silver, forgetting how miserable clay is compared to those precious and enduring metals (15:9). Not surprisingly, ignorance is the root cause of the folly. The potter is satisfied with the inert clay only because "he knew not the one who . . . breathed into him a quickening soul" (15:11). Some vessels are for ignoble purposes, whereas others are for noble uses; the final arbiter of value is the very human being who is also made from clay (15:7)! The ultimate driving force for the whole

[10]Ashes his heart is! more worthless
    than earth is his hope,
    more ignoble than clay his life;
[11]Because he knew not the one who
    fashioned him,
    and breathed into him a quicken-
        ing soul,
    and infused a vital spirit.
[12]Instead, he esteemed our life a mere
    game,
    and our span of life a holiday for
        gain;
"For one must," says he, "make a
    profit in every way, be it even
    from evil."
[13]For more than anyone else he knows
    that he is sinning,
    when out of earthen stuff he
        creates fragile vessels and
        idols alike.

[14]But most stupid of all and worse
    than senseless in mind,
    are the enemies of your people
        who enslaved them.
[15]For they esteemed all the idols of
    the nations as gods,
    which cannot use their eyes to
        see,
    nor nostrils to breathe the air,
Nor ears to hear,
    nor fingers on their hands for
        feeling;
    even their feet are useless to walk
        with.
[16]For it was a mere human being who
    made them;
    one living on borrowed breath
        who fashioned them.
For no one is able to fashion a god
    like himself;

---

industry of image making is greed born of the conviction that life has no meaning (15:12). Money determines all. The underlying desperation recalls the attitude of the malicious gang in Wisdom 2:1-9 and 5:8-14. How can such clay figures ever represent the God who created and sustains the entire universe!

15:14-19 The Egyptians, enemies of God's people, venerators of images and animals

The third group, the Egyptians, also failed to know God. They are the worst of all, for they not only adopted other nations' images, but worshiped animals and were "enemies of your people who enslaved them" (15:14b). The epithet applied to them, *aphronestatoi*, "most stupid of all" (v. 14a), is the most biting of all. Like the "foolish" philosophers (13:1-9) and the wretched image venerators (15:10-13), the "most stupid of all " Egyptians are another instance of the ignorant gang that attacked the child of God in chapter 2. None of these three groups truly *knows* God; they think God is materially within creation, or in inert images, or in living animals. The last group does not know God is with the chosen people. The so-called digression is thus thematically related to Part 1 of the book.

¹⁷he is mortal, and what he makes
with lawless hands is dead.
For he is better than the things he
worships;
he at least lives, but never his
idols.

Second Example Resumed

¹⁸Besides, they worship the most
loathsome beasts—

as regards stupidity, these are
worse than the rest,
¹⁹For beasts are neither good-looking
nor desirable;
they have escaped both the
approval of God and his
blessing.

16 ¹Therefore they were fittingly
punished by similar creatures,
and were tormented by a swarm
of insects.

The author makes no attempt to understand Egyptian religion sympathetically (nor the other religions in the book, for that matter). Wisdom of Solomon is a tract in the Hellenistic marketplace of ideas: criticize other religions, uphold your own. A defender of image worship might say that the image presents an aspect of the deity without containing it; its aim is to facilitate an encounter between deity and worshiper. The author, however, concentrates only on the dangers of such worship, and attributes the depravity of worshipers to their images.

The mention of image worship returns the reader to 11:15-16, which provoked the digression in the first place, where it is said that the Egyptians were punished for worshiping unknowing serpents and worthless insects. God sent them swarms of unknowing animals in punishment.

Comparisons of Egyptians and
Israelites during the Exodus (11:1-14; 16:1–19:22)

The digressions on divine retribution (11:15–12:27) and on false worship (Wis 13–15) have come to an end. The mention of animals in 15:18-19 brings the reader back to the animals (gnats and frogs) of the exodus plagues. The author returns to the exodus, which is presented in the form of seven comparisons. The principle of divine activity that operates in the comparisons has already been stated in 11:5: the act that benefits Israel punishes their foes. Actually, the principle has been operative in the book from its very beginning, for the death of the just person meant entry into eternal life and death for the killers (chs. 2 and 5).

16:1-4 Comparison two: frogs and quails

The critique of animal worship in 15:18-19 provides a transition to the animal passage in 16:1-4. Wisdom 16:1-4 repeats words from the first com-

*The rod of Asclepius, a staff entwined with a serpent, has been a symbol of the
physician since antiquity. See Wisdom 16:5-7 and Numbers 21:4-9.*

²Instead of this punishment, you benefited your people
with a novel dish, the delight they craved,
by providing quail for their food,
³So that those others, when they desired food,
should lose their appetite even for necessities,
since the creatures sent to plague them were so loathsome,
While these, after a brief period of privation,
partook of a novel dish.
⁴For inexorable want had to come upon those oppressors;
but these needed only to be shown how their enemies were being tormented.
⁵For when the dire venom of beasts came upon them ▶
and they were dying from the bite of crooked serpents,
your anger endured not to the end.
⁶But as a warning, for a short time they were terrorized,
though they had a sign of salvation, to remind them of the precept of your law.
⁷For the one who turned toward it was saved,

parison in 11:1-4, alerting the reader that the comparisons are starting up again, e.g., "punished" in 16:1 and 11:8, 16; "tormented" in 16:1 and 11:9; "swarms" in 16:1 and 11:15, 17; "benefit" in 16:2 and 11:5, 13.

The feeding of the people with quails is told in Exodus 16:13 (in a story otherwise concerned only with manna) and in Numbers 11 where the quail is given to the people dissatisfied with manna. In the Pentateuch and in Psalm 78:26-31 (though not in Ps 105:40), the quails are a curse rather than a blessing, for they bring a plague. Wisdom of Solomon regards it as a pure blessing. The author combines the exodus plagues of small animals, frogs (plague two, Exod 8:1-15), gnats (plague three, Exod 8:16-19), flies (plague four, Exod 8:20-32), and locusts (plague eight, Exod 10:1-20).

The themes of the first comparison are continued. The same thing brings punishment to the ungodly and benefit to God's people. The animals of the Egyptians are too loathsome to eat, whereas the animals of the Israelites, the quails, satisfy their hunger. The brief hunger that Israel felt (Wis 10:3d) is only to remind them of the gnawing want their enemies must endure. God is shown to be utter master of creation, playing it like an instrument (see 5:17-23) to ensure that the divine will is done (see 19:18-22).

16:5-14 Comparison three: flies/locusts and the bronze serpent

The third comparison is developed with considerable freedom. It emphasizes the bronze serpent, which Israelites who had been bitten by

not by what was seen,
but by you, the savior of all.
⁸By this also you convinced our
foes
that you are the one who delivers
from all evil.
⁹For the bites of locusts and of flies
slew them,
and no remedy was found to
save their lives
because they deserved to be
punished by such means;
¹⁰But not even the fangs of
poisonous reptiles overcame
your children,
for your mercy came forth and
healed them.

¹¹For as a reminder of your injunc-
tions, they were stung,
and swiftly they were saved,
Lest they should fall into deep
forgetfulness
and become unresponsive to
your beneficence.
¹²For indeed, neither herb nor appli-
cation cured them,
but your all-healing word,
O LORD!
¹³For you have dominion over life
and death;
you lead down to the gates of
Hades and lead back.
¹⁴Human beings, however, may kill
another with malice,

poisonous serpents had only to look on to be healed (Wis 16:5-8, 10-11). In contrast, flies (plague four, Exod 8:20-32) and locusts (plague eight, Exod 10:1-20) slew the Egyptians and no remedy was found to save their lives (Wis 16:9). The author is careful to state that those looking upon the bronze serpent were saved not by what they saw, "but by you, the savior of all" (16:7 and see vv. 12-13, 15).

The basis of this treatment is Numbers 21:4-9, the last of the complaint stories in the wilderness journey to the promised land. The people accused the Lord as well as Moses of bringing them into the wilderness to kill them by depriving them of food and water. The Lord sends poisonous serpents to punish them, the people cry out, Moses intercedes successfully, and the Lord provides a solution—a bronze image of a poisonous serpent. Those bitten had only to look at it to be healed. Serpents were associated with healing in antiquity; even today the caduceus, a representation of a staff with two entwined serpents and wings at the top, is a symbol of a physician. Wisdom of Solomon omits any mention of the rebellion that made the bronze serpent a necessary remedy, concentrating exclusively on its healing (Wis 16:10a). The author interprets the whole episode as a teaching moment, an instance of "discipline" in the terminology of wisdom literature. The Israelites were terrorized "for a short time" (16:6) purely for an educational purpose—to make them aware of divine salvation (16:6 and 11). The bronze serpent is a perfect foil to the locusts and flies whose bites killed the Egyptians.

but they cannot bring back the
departed spirit,
or release the soul that death has
confined.
¹⁵Your hand no one can escape.

**Third Example:
A Rain of Manna for Israel Instead of
the Plague of Storms**

¹⁶For the wicked who refused to
know you
were punished by the might of
your arm,
Were pursued by unusual rains and
hailstorms and unremitting
downpours,
and were consumed by fire.

¹⁷For against all expectation, in water
which quenches everything,
the fire grew more active;
For the universe fights on behalf of
the righteous.
¹⁸Then the flame was tempered
so that the beasts that were sent
upon the wicked might
not be burnt up,
but that these might see and know
that they were struck by the
judgment of God;
¹⁹And again, even in the water, fire
blazed beyond its strength
so as to consume the produce of
the wicked land.
²⁰Instead of this, you nourished your
people with food of angels

Once again, God uses creation with utter freedom to bring about justice. By one and the same means—animals—the wicked are punished and the righteous are rewarded.

16:15-29 Comparison four: storm/hail and manna

Thunder and hail constitute the seventh plague in Exodus 8:13-35. As the previous comparison began with the benefit to Israel (the bronze serpent), this one begins with the punishment of Egypt, the thunderstorm (Wis 16:16-19, 22). The story concentrates on only one element of the storm, lightning (Exod 9:23, 24), which it calls "fire." The Hebrew word can mean both fire and lightning. Why concentrate on "fire"? Because fire provides the author with an opportunity to show how God changes the nature of things for the sake of justice. Despite the water of the thunderstorm, the fire was intensified (Wis 16:17), but was prevented from destroying the beasts already sent to punish. Wisdom 16:18, which presumes the animals were sent simultaneously rather than successively, is contrary to the Exodus account. The fire was again intensified to destroy Egyptian crops (16:19), but lessened so as not to harm the food of Israel (16:22). The alteration of the nature of fire shows that it is "your word that preserves those who believe in you" (16:26). The author is, as ever, careful to show that God uses created elements but is not identified with them.

and furnished them bread from
heaven, ready to hand,
untoiled-for,
endowed with all delights and
conforming to every taste.
²¹For this substance of yours
revealed your sweetness
toward your children,
and serving the desire of the one
who received it,
was changed to whatever flavor
each one wished.
²²Yet snow and ice withstood fire and
were not melted,
so that they might know that
their enemies' fruits

Were consumed by a fire that blazed
in the hail
and flashed lightning in the rain.

²³But this fire, again, in order that the
righteous might be nourished,
forgot even its proper strength;
²⁴For your creation, serving you, its
maker,
grows tense for punishment
against the wicked,
but is relaxed in benefit for those
who trust in you.
²⁵Therefore at that very time, transformed in all sorts of ways,
it was serving your all-nourishing
bounty

The passage begins with the storm that none could escape and that devastated the produce of the land (16:15-19). According to Exodus 9:26, only the land of Goshen, where the Hebrews lived, was spared. That detail seems to have suggested to the author the contrast between the destroyed food ("the produce," Wis 16:19b) of Egypt and the protected food ("food of angels," 16:20) of Israel. Fire destroys the one (v. 19), but not the other (v. 22). The author expands the biblical depiction of manna, asserting that it was capable of taking on any taste (vv. 20-21). "Snow and ice" in verse 22 refers to the manna; it uses the figure of hendiadys (literally, one meaning through two words), "icy snow." Manna is also called snow in Wisdom 16:27 and 19:21. The metaphor comes from Exodus 16:14 where manna is "fine flakes like hoarfrost." In the somewhat strained connection, the author wants readers to marvel at the fire that destroyed the produce of Egypt's land, but left unharmed the ice-like manna, the food of "your children" (16:21a). Writers of the time compared manna to snow, (e.g., Josephus, *Antiquities* 3.1.6). The preservation of the manna from harm also had an instructional purpose, for it reminded Israel that their enemies' food was destroyed (16:22). Verse 24 seeks to explain philosophically the miracle of the fire that burned in water and of the ice-like manna that did not melt in fire. The language about creation being tense and relaxed derives ultimately from Plato, *Republic* 442A and *Phaedo* 86C, 94C and was current among the Stoics. According to the doctrine, the elements of fire and water were

according to what they needed
and desired;
26That your children whom you
loved might learn, O LORD,
that it is not the various kinds of
fruits that nourish,
but your word that preserves
those who believe you!
27For what was not destroyed by fire,
melted when merely warmed by
a momentary sunbeam;
28To make known that one must give
you thanks before sunrise,
and turn to you at daybreak.
29For the hope of the ungrateful melts
like a wintry frost
and runs off like useless water.

**Fourth Example:
Darkness Afflicts the Egyptians,
While the Israelites Have Light**

17 1For great are your judgments,
and hard to describe;
therefore the unruly souls went
astray.

2For when the lawless thought to
enslave the holy nation,
they themselves lay shackled
with darkness, fettered by
the long night,
confined beneath their own roofs
as exiles from the eternal
providence.
3For they, who supposed their secret
sins were hid
under the dark veil of oblivion,
Were scattered in fearful trembling,
terrified by apparitions.
4For not even their inner chambers
kept them unafraid,
for crashing sounds on all sides
terrified them,
and mute phantoms with somber
looks appeared.
5No fire had force enough to give
light,
nor did the flaming brilliance of
the stars
succeed in lighting up that
gloomy night.
6But only intermittent, fearful fires

transformed by the heightening or lowering of their inherent "tension" (Greek *tonos*); the result was that their usual properties did not appear. Wisdom 16:26 adapts Deuteronomy 8:3 (see Matt 4:4): "[God] therefore let you be afflicted with hunger, and then fed you with manna . . . in order to show you that not by bread alone does man live, but by every word that comes forth from the mouth of the LORD." In another elaboration of the biblical data, Wisdom 16:27 declares that the manna not collected on one day did not remain for the next day because it melted by a single sunbeam.

17:1–18:4 Comparison five: darkness and light

In Exodus 10:21-29 the ninth plague is darkness over all the land of Egypt for three days, though the Israelites had light where they lived. Exodus 10:21 says there was "such intense darkness that one can feel it" and Exodus 10:23 adds that people "could not see one another, nor could they move from where they were."

flashed through upon them;
And in their terror they thought
    beholding these was worse
    than the times when that sight
        was no longer to be seen.
⁷And mockeries of their magic art
    failed,
    and there was a humiliating
        refutation of their
        vaunted shrewdness.
⁸For they who undertook to banish
    fears and terrors from the
    sick soul
    themselves sickened with ridic-
        ulous fear.
⁹For even though no monstrous thing
    frightened them,
    they shook at the passing of
        insects and the hissing of
        reptiles,
¹⁰And perished trembling,
    reluctant to face even the air that
        they could nowhere escape.
¹¹For wickedness, of its nature
    cowardly, testifies in its own
    condemnation,

and because of a distressed con-
    science, always magnifies
    misfortunes.
¹²For fear is nought but the surrender
    of the helps that come from
    reason;
¹³and the more one's expectation
    is of itself uncertain,
    the more one makes of not
        knowing the cause that
        brings on torment.
¹⁴So they, during that night, power-
    less though it was,
    since it had come upon them
        from the recesses of a
        powerless Hades,
    while all sleeping the same sleep,
¹⁵Were partly smitten by fearsome
    apparitions
    and partly stricken by their souls'
        surrender;
    for fear overwhelmed them,
        sudden and unexpected.
¹⁶Thus, then, whoever was there fell
    into that prison without bars and
        was kept confined.

Wisdom of Solomon expands these details in an elaborate antithesis between the Egyptians and the Israelites. It imagines Israel's captors themselves imprisoned in their dark chambers and terrified by strange noises (18:2-4). They are unable to light a fire to ward off the darkness (17:5). The only lights were momentary bursts which, when they subsided, left people more terrified than before (17:6). The description moves subtly to the psychological effects of darkness—loss of confidence by people who previously had great faith in their spiritual powers (17:7-8) and fear in every aspect of their lives (17:9-10). The author asks why fear spread so quickly and completely through the Egyptian community and answers that their wickedness made them vulnerable (17:11-12). Thick night took away their senses and made them subject to self-imagined terrors, locking them in a prison without bars (17:13-16). People of every class of society (even those who had fled to the desert from debts and hardships, 17:17b) were afflicted so that the pleasant sounds of wind and of birds or the brutal sounds of beasts

¹⁷For whether one was a farmer, or
a shepherd,
or a worker at tasks in the
wasteland,
Taken unawares, each served out the
inescapable sentence;
¹⁸for all were bound by the one
bond of darkness.
And were it only the whistling
wind,
or the melodious song of birds in
the spreading branches,
Or the steady sound of rushing water,
¹⁹or the rude crash of overthrown
rocks,
Or the unseen gallop of bounding
animals,
or the roaring cry of the fiercest
beasts,
Or an echo resounding from the
hollow of the hills—
these sounds, inspiring terror,
paralyzed them.
²⁰For the whole world shone with
brilliant light
and continued its works without
interruption;
²¹But over them alone was spread
oppressive night,
an image of the darkness that was
about to come upon them.
Yet they were more a burden to
themselves than was the
darkness.

---

inspired terror equally (17:17-19). Only the Egyptians had to endure darkness and its psychological devastation; the rest of the world went happily about its business, bathed in light (17:20-21).

After a lengthy description of the punishment inflicted on Egypt, the author turns to Israel (18:1-4) who enjoyed the natural light of day, the flaming fire by night ("the flaming pillar" in v. 3; see Exod 13:21), and, in climactic third place, "the imperishable light of the law" (18:4c). Israel, "your holy ones," enjoyed brilliant light so that even the Egyptians recognized they were favored and called them blest (18:1-2). Verse 4 sums up the comparison—the captors become captives, the captives escape, all this happening through divine mastery over the element of light. There is a deeper divine purpose, that the imperishable light of the law should be given to the world through the agency of Israel (v. 4c).

The promise that the light of the law would be made available to the nations is found in the Bible as early as Isaiah 2:3-4 (= Mic 4:2-3), "Come, let us go up to the LORD's mountain, / to the house of the God of Jacob, / That he may instruct us in his ways, / and we may walk in his paths. / For from Zion shall go forth instruction, / and the word of the LORD from Jerusalem." In the ancient Near East, the sun was hailed as the god of justice. Psalm 19 implicitly compares the torah to the sun, and Sirach 24:32 says that wisdom is found in the torah and shines forth like the dawn. Jewish-Hellenistic and rabbinic literature speak of Israel's obligation to bring the torah to the nations, e.g., Testament of Levi 14:4; 2 Baruch 48:40; 59:2. In-

18 ¹But your holy ones had very
great light;
And those others, who heard their
voices but did not see their
forms,
counted them blest for not having
suffered;
²And because they who formerly
had been wronged did not
harm them, they thanked
them,
and because of the difference
between them, pleaded
with them.
³Instead of this, you furnished the
flaming pillar,
a guide on the unknown way,
and the mild sun for an honorable
migration.

⁴For they deserved to be deprived
of light and imprisoned by
darkness,
they had kept your children
confined,
through whom the imperishable
light of the law was to be
given to the world.

**Fifth Example:
Death of the Egyptian Firstborn;
the Israelites Are Spared**

⁵When they determined to put to
death the infants of the holy
ones,
and when a single boy had
been cast forth and then
saved,

spired by a universalistic conception of the human race rooted in Hellenistic and biblical ideals, Philo believed Israel to be a model for other nations and its law to be "a law for the world" (*Questions and Answers on Exodus* 2.42).

Wisdom of Solomon develops the biblical story with great rhetorical skill and originality. The story of the plague of darkness is enriched by psychological observation and broadened by symbols of light and darkness.

18:5-25 Comparison six: death of the Egyptian first born and the sparing of Israel

The first-born child plays a large role in the book of Exodus. After the call of Moses in Exodus 3–4, the Lord tells Moses to perform wonders before Pharaoh and say, "Let my son go, that he may serve me. Since you refused to let him go, I will kill your son, your first-born" (Exod 4:23). The high god was thought to have a claim on one's firstborn. One either sacrificed one's child directly or, as in biblical narratives (Gen 22:1-19) and legislation (e.g., Exod 13:1-16; 34:19-20), offered an animal in its place. Exodus 11–12 interpret the killing of the Egyptian first-born as both poetic justice for Pharaoh's refusal to "let my son go" and as an act of obeisance to the Lord.

Wisdom of Solomon interprets the tenth and climactic plague much differently. It sets it within the comparisons: (1) as the Egyptians tried to

As a reproof you carried off a
  multitude of their children
and made them perish all at once
  in the mighty water.
⁶That night was known beforehand
  to our ancestors,
so that, with sure knowledge of
  the oaths in which they
  put their faith, they might
  have courage.
⁷The expectation of your people
  was the salvation of the righteous
  and the destruction of
  their foes.
⁸For by the same means with which
  you punished our adversar-
  ies,
  you glorified us whom you had
  summoned.
⁹For in secret the holy children of the
  good were offering sacrifice
and carried out with one mind
  the divine institution,
So that your holy ones should share
  alike the same blessings and
  dangers,
once they had sung the ancestral
  hymns of praise.

¹⁰But the discordant cry of their
  enemies echoed back,
and the piteous wail of mourning
  for children was borne to
  them.
¹¹And the slave was smitten with the
  same retribution as the master;
even the commoner suffered the
  same as the king.
¹²And all alike by one common form
  of death
had countless dead;
For the living were not even suffi-
  cient for the burial,
since at a single instant their
  most valued offspring
  had been destroyed.
¹³For though they disbelieved at
  every turn on account of
  sorceries,
at the destruction of the first-
  born they acknowledged
  that this people was
  God's son.
¹⁴For when peaceful stillness en-
  compassed everything
and the night in its swift course
  was half spent,

put to death the infants of the Israelites, God in punishment killed their children (Wis 18:5); (2) the Israelites interpreted it as "the salvation of the righteous and the destruction of their foes" (18:7); (3) God's all-powerful word killed the Egyptian first-born (18:15-19), whereas the plague that briefly touched Israel in the wilderness was stopped by the righteous Aaron (18:20-25).

Moses is the "boy" (Greek *teknon*, Wis 18:5) who is cast off and rescued yet saves his people like the wisdom-endowed individuals in chapter 10. The same Greek word is used for the Israelites in 16:21 (*tekna*, "children"). The "sworn covenants with their ancestors" (18:22) are the promises made to the patriarchs in Genesis, especially those in which God promises to be their God (e.g., Gen 17:8) and be *with* them (e.g., Gen 26:3; 31:3; cf. Ps 105:42-43). "In secret" in Wisdom 18:9 has occasioned much comment. Most prob-

¹⁵Your all-powerful word from
heaven's royal throne
leapt into the doomed land,
¹⁶a fierce warrior bearing the
sharp sword of your
inexorable decree,
And alighted, and filled every place
with death,
and touched heaven, while standing upon the earth.
¹⁷Then, at once, visions in horrible
dreams perturbed them
and unexpected fears assailed
them;
¹⁸And cast half-dead, one here,
another there,
they revealed why they were
dying.
¹⁹For the dreams that disturbed them
had proclaimed this beforehand,
lest they perish unaware of why
they endured such evil.

²⁰The trial of death touched even the
righteous,
and in the desert a plague struck
the multitude;
Yet not for long did the anger last.

²¹For the blameless man hastened to
be their champion,
bearing the weapon of his special
office,
prayer and the propitiation of
incense;
He withstood the wrath and put a
stop to the calamity,
showing that he was your servant.
²²He overcame the bitterness
not by bodily strength, not by
force of arms;
But by word he overcame the smiter,
recalling the sworn covenants
with their ancestors.
²³For when corpses had already fallen
one on another in heaps,
he stood in the midst and checked
the anger,
and cut off its way to the living.
²⁴For on his full-length robe was the
whole world,
and ancestral glories were carved
on the four rows of stones,
and your grandeur was on the
crown upon his head.
²⁵To these the destroyer yielded,
these he feared;
for this sole trial of anger sufficed.

---

ably, it suggests that Israel was already carrying out the rituals of Passover; "the ancestral hymn of praise " refers to the Egyptian Hallel (Psalms 113–118) sung before and after the Passover meal (cf. Matt 26:30 and Mark 14:26). The Egyptians' acknowledgment in Wisdom 18:13 "that this people was God's son" refers back to Wisdom 2 and 5 where the just person afflicted by the wicked is rescued by God and elicits the admission, "See how he is accounted among the heavenly beings!" (5:5). The impressive description of the descent of the all-powerful word from heaven's throne in 18:14-16 may owe something to classical descriptions of Athena leaping from the brow of Zeus. It also resembles the description of the powerful word of God in Hebrews 4:12.

"The blameless man" in 18:21 is Aaron, whose offering of incense among the people saved the people from the plague that was just beginning (Num

19 ¹But merciless wrath assailed the
wicked until the end,
for God knew beforehand what
they were yet to do:
²That though they themselves had
agreed to the departure
and had anxiously sent them on
their way,

they would regret it and pursue
them.
³For while they were still engaged
in funeral rites
and mourning at the burials of
the dead,
They adopted another senseless
plan:

17:6-15): "standing there between the living and the dead. And so the scourge was checked" (Num 17:13). The reference to Aaron's robe on which was emblazoned the whole world, and the glories of the fathers carved in four rows upon the stones (Wis 18:24) elaborate Exodus 28, which is concerned with the vestments of the chief priest (Aaron). Exodus 28:9-10 prescribes that the ephod (a long vest) have two onyx stones inscribed with the names of the sons of Israel in the order of their birth, and Exodus 28:15-21 prescribes that the "breastpiece of decision" (a purse holding sacred lots) have four rows of stones inscribed with the names of the sons of Israel, i.e., the twelve tribes. The "crown" in Wisdom 18:24c, described in Exodus 28:36-38, is a golden rosette attached to the front of the high priest's turban. The priest represents the people and carries them into the presence of the Lord. The inscribed names of the tribes are sufficiently powerful to make the instigator of the desert plague flee; to disturb further the holy children would incur divine wrath (Wis 18:25). The phrase "on his full-length robe was [depicted] the whole world" (18:24) represents a Stoic-Cynic idea that the universe is a temple. Philo also has the idea in *On the Life of Moses* 2:117-135; Josephus mentions it in *Antiquities* 3:7.7; 3.7.5: the priestly robe is a likeness and copy of the universe, and the twelve stones reflect the zodiac symbolizing the four seasons, so that the high priest carries an image of the All.

The emphasis is on death of the Egyptian firstborn as retaliation for the attempt to kill the infant Moses. The holy priest Aaron stopped the incipient plague in the wilderness, but no one could stop the horrible plague in Egypt. Thus does God control the universe to punish the wicked and reward the just.

19:1-9 Comparison seven: drowning of the Egyptian in the Red Sea and the passage of Israel through the Red Sea

Exodus 14–15 tells of Israel's flight through the Red Sea and the drowning of the Egyptian pursuers. The Egyptians, at first numb from the death

The Red Sea covers the Egyptians who are in pursuit of the Israelites. "Your people might experience a glorious journey while the others met an extraordinary death" (Wisdom 19:5).

those whom they had driven out
with entreaties
they now pursued as fugitives.
⁴For a compulsion appropriate to
this ending drew them on,
and made them forget what had
befallen them,
That they might complete the torments of their punishment,
⁵and your people might experience a glorious journey
while those others met an extraordinary death.

⁶For all creation, in its several
kinds, was being made
over anew,
serving your commands,
that your children

might be preserved un-
harmed.
⁷The cloud overshadowed their
camp;
and out of what had been water,
dry land was seen emerg-
ing:
Out of the Red Sea an unimpeded
road,
and a grassy plain out of the
mighty flood.
⁸Over this crossed the whole nation
sheltered by your hand,
and they beheld stupendous
wonders.
⁹For they ranged about like horses,
and leapt like lambs,
praising you, LORD, their
deliverer.

---

of their children, begged the Israelites to leave. Changing their minds, they pursued them, only to be struck down by the massive waters obedient to the Lord's command. In Wisdom 19:1-9, the antithesis of Egypt and Israel is not sharply drawn; the reader is left to infer the drowning of the Egyptians from verses 3-5. There are two emphases. One is the marvelous crossing and subsequent journey of "your children" (19:6), and the other is "a compulsion" (19:4; Greek *anagkē*, lit. "necessity") that drove the Egyptians to self-destruction. The author needs only to remind the reader that the principle of poetic justice is part and parcel of the holy people's history, and that creation preserves "your children unharmed" (19:6) as promised in 5:16-23 and 19:18-22. The people "ranged about like horses, and bounded about like lambs" (19:9), a reference to Psalm 114:3-4, which celebrates the crossing of the Red Sea, "the Jordan turned back. / The mountains skipped like rams; / the hills, like lambs."

In the seventh and final comparison, the Egyptians are finished as a threat to the holy people, for their young are destroyed (18:5-25) and their army wiped out (19:1-5). The Israelites are on their way to the promised land (19:7-9). There remains only a summary and an explicit statement that the experience of the exodus generation will be the experience of Israel for all future time.

¹⁰For they were still mindful of
what had happened in their
sojourn:
how instead of the young of
animals the land brought
forth gnats,
and instead of fishes the river
swarmed with countless
frogs.
¹¹And later they saw also a new kind
of bird
when, prompted by desire, they
asked for pleasant foods;
¹²For to appease them quail came to
them from the sea.
¹³And the punishments came upon
the sinners

not without forewarnings from
the violence of the thun-
derbolts.

For they justly suffered for their
own misdeeds,
since they treated their guests
with the more grievous
hatred.
¹⁴For those others did not receive
unfamiliar visitors,
but these were enslaving benefi-
cent guests.
¹⁵And not that only; but what punishment was to be theirs
since they received strangers
unwillingly!

19:10-22 Summary of the history, final critique of the wicked (Egyptians), and the statement that God glorifies his people at all times and places

The people now remember ("were still mindful," v. 10) the reversal of expectations in Egypt and the wilderness. Instead of the young of animals, the land produced gnats; instead of fishes, the river produced frogs; and the wilderness produced a new kind of bird, the quail from the sea. The comments generalize the specific reversals, implying that they are only a harbinger of the alterations of nature that will be made for the holy people. The author uses a favorite word "instead of" (*anti*) twice in verse 10 (cf. 7:10: 11:6, 15; 16:2, 20; 18:3).

Non-Jewish Hellenistic writers such as Diodorus and Hecataeus of Abdera accused the Jews of hatred of humankind on the grounds that they kept themselves apart by dietary laws and other customs. The Jewish philosopher Philo responded with spirit to these charges and, like Wisdom of Solomon, threw the charge back to the Egyptians (*On the Life of Moses* 1:36). Wisdom 19:13-17 does the same, comparing the Egyptians with the men of Sodom who attempted to rape the two angelic strangers despite their being under the protection of Lot. In punishment the men were struck with blindness and their city was destroyed (Gen 19). The men of Sodom come off much better than the Egyptians, for the latter at least were dealing with

¹⁶Yet these, after welcoming them
with festivities,
oppressed with awful toils
those who had shared with them
the same rights.
¹⁷And they were struck with blindness,
as those others had been at the
doors of the righteous
man—
When, surrounded by yawning
darkness,
each sought the entrance of his
own door.
¹⁸For the elements, in ever-changing
harmony,
like strings of the harp, produce
new melody,
while the flow of music steadily
persists.
And this can be perceived exactly
from a review of what took
place.
¹⁹For land creatures were changed
into water creatures,
and those that swam went over
on land.
²⁰Fire in water maintained its own
strength,
and water forgot its quenching
nature;
²¹Flames, by contrast, neither consumed the flesh

---

strangers, people they did not know (Wis 19:13-15). The Egyptians, in contrast, knew the Israelites full well, had profited from their work (Gen 41:37-
57; 47:13-26), and had earlier welcomed them (Gen 47:1-12). They were
without excuse, therefore, and rightly suffered the blindness inflicted also
on the men of Sodom (Wis 19:17; cf. Gen 19:11; Exod 14:20). In keeping with
the typifying tendency in the book, the acts are not named.

The last section of the book (vv. 18-21) expresses the wondrous guidance
of God's people in the language of Stoic cosmology, as Stoicism and Epicureanism were also ways of life, and had explanations of the physical
world (cosmologies) from which ethical principles were derived. Wisdom
19:18 apparently uses an analogy from music (varying the key while holding to the melody) to illustrate how elements within the universe can be
altered without interrupting the orderly functioning of the universe. According to the Stoic cosmology (already referred to in 16:24), the tension
(*tonos*) of the elements was heightened or lowered affecting their make-up,
just as the tension of a musical mode is varied by the notes within it. Philo
of Alexandria uses similar argumentation in describing the miracle of
manna, claiming that the heavenly food, like the created world, was begun
by God on the first of six days. As God called up his most perfect work, the
world, out of non-being into being, so he called up abundance in the desert,
changing the elements (see Wis 19:18a) to meet the pressing need of the
occasion (*On the Life of Moses* 2:266-267).

of the perishable animals that
went about in them,
nor melted the icelike, quick-
melting kind of ambrosial
food.

²²For every way, Lord! you magnified
and glorified your people;
unfailing, you stood by them in
every time and circum-
stance.

Verses 19-21 illustrate the transposition of elements: "land creatures were changed into water creatures" refers to the Israelites crossing through the Red Sea (Exod 14–15 and Wis 19:1-9); "those that swam" were the frogs (Exod 8:1-15 and Wis 16:1-4); "fire" is the author's term for lightning that burned the Egyptians even in water (Exod 9:23-24; Wis 16:17); "flames" that spared and were gentle refers to Wisdom 16:18, 22.

The final verse is a doxology (a formula giving praise to God), common in Jewish religious literature and at the end of wisdom books. Each of the five books of the Psalter ends with a doxology (Pss 41:14; 72:18-19; 89:53; 106:48; 150). The verse is also a fine summary of the book.

REVIEW AIDS AND DISCUSSION TOPICS

Introduction to the Book of Wisdom *(pages 5–14)*

1. What do we know about the author of Wisdom of Solomon?

2. What role does the author give to Solomon, King of Israel? Why?

3. What influences from Hellenistic religion and philosophy are discernible in the book?

4. At first glance, the sections of the book seem independent of each other. Can you show how they are united?

5. What is the relevance of the book today for Christian readers?

1:1–6:21 The Two Worlds *(pages 15–31)*

1. What is meant by "justice" and "wisdom" in the two "bookend" sections of 1:1-11 and 6:1-21?

2. How is the typical scene in chapter 2, the righteous person attacked by the wicked gang, related to the rest of the book?

3. What is the author's main point in chapters 3–4 about the relative merits of childlessness and having many children?

4. What is the context for the judgment scene in chapter 5?

5. What is the meaning of the Lord putting on armor at the end of chapter 5?

6:22–10:21 Wisdom and the Way to It *(pages 31–46)*

1. Why in chapter 7 does the author put such stress on Solomon being so much like us?

2. How do you explain the fact that wisdom needs to be earnestly striven for and yet is a completely gracious gift of God?

3. What are the motives given in chapter 8 for acquiring wisdom? Do these have any meaning for today?

4. Explain how wisdom can be both a quality of God and a characteristic of human beings.

5. Chapter 10 interprets history as events guided by wisdom-inspired individuals. Can you think of other biblical ways of interpreting history?

11–19 The Exodus: God Provides for His Child Israel *(pages 46–85)*

1. Why does the author focus exclusively on the exodus in attempting to show how Israel is divinely guided?

2. Why does the author insist so strongly that Israel is benefited and its enemies punished by the same event?

3. Does the topic of the first digression—God's patience in dealing with sinners—seem to you to be related to the other topics?

4. What is the relation of the second digression—false ways of worshiping—to the other topics?

5. Are you able to follow the ways in which the author elaborates the events of the exodus through elaborating on well-known stories?

6. Do you think the book succeeds in showing that God controls nature as well as history? Do you think that the book has something to say about the value of the natural environment?

INDEX OF CITATIONS FROM THE
CATECHISM OF THE CATHOLIC CHURCH

The arabic number(s) following the citation refer(s) to the paragraph number(s) in the *Catechism of the Catholic Church*. The asterisk following a paragraph number indicates that the citation has been paraphrased.

Wisdom

1:13	413, 1008*	8:2	2500	13:1-15, 19	2112*
2:23-24	1008*	8:7	1805	13:1-9	32,* 216*
2:24	391,* 413, 2538*	9:9	295*	13:1	1147*
4:8	1308	10:5	57*	13:3	2129, 2500
7:16-17	2501*	11:20	299	13:5	41, 2500
7:17-21	216,* 283	11:21	269	14:12	2534*
7:25-26	2500	11:23	269	15:5	2520
7:29-30	2500	11:24-26	301	16:5-14	2130*
8:1	302	11:24	373	18:13	441*